Teaching Patients With Low Literacy Skills

Cecilia Conrath Doak, M.P.H.
Director of Education
Patient Learning Associates, Inc.
Potomac, Maryland

Leonard G. Doak, B.S., P.E.
President
Patient Learning Associates, Inc.
Potomac, Maryland

Jane H. Root, Ph.D.
Professor of Reading Education (Retired)
Johnson State College
Johnson, Vermont

A DAVID T. MILLER BOOK

Teaching Patients With Low Literacy Skills

J.B. LIPPINCOTT COMPANY   Philadelphia
London   Mexico City   New York   St. Louis   São Paulo   Sydney

Sponsoring Editor: David T. Miller
Manuscript Editor: Elizabeth P. Lowe
Indexer: Carol M. Kosik
Design Director: Tracy Baldwin
Designer: Earl Gerhart
Production Supervisor: J. Corey Gray
Production Coordinator: Don Wilby
Compositor: McFarland Graphics & Design, Inc.
Printer/Binder: R.R. Donnelley & Sons Company
Cover Printer: Phillips Offset

6   5   4   3

Library of Congress Cataloging in Publication Data

Doak, Cecilia Conrath.
   Teaching patients with low literacy skills.

   Bibliography: p.
   Includes index.
   1. Patient education.   2. Illiteracy.   3. Nurse and
patient.   I. Doak, Leonard G.   II. Root, Jane H.
III. Title.   [DNLM: 1. Educational Status.   2. Patient
Education—methods.   W 85 D63lt]
RT90.D63   1985   613'.07   84-15400
ISBN 0-397-54498-7

*To the unsung heroes in the health field
who are working to get their messages across to
patients with low literacy skills.*

FOREWORD

The scope of the problem of illiteracy was dramatically brought home to me a number of years ago by a patient on one of our wards. Every morning he and his roommate bought the *New York Times*, and every morning they remained engrossed in the papers for at least two hours. Then, on the day of his discharge, an astute nurse discovered that this patient couldn't read a word! An incident like this—apparently so unlikely— makes one wonder how many times health professionals have completely overlooked patients' poor or nonexistent reading skills as they taught them using printed materials.

Shortly after this happened, I joined the staff of the Diabetes Project of the North Carolina Regional Medical Program. As part of our effort to improve diabetes education in the state, we asked health professionals what kind of help they needed most. One of the loudest cries for help was for teaching materials for patients with low literacy skills. When an extensive search showed that almost no such materials existed, we devoted ourselves to developing some.

Several years later I received a frantic call for help from the staff of the National Diabetes Information Clearinghouse. They were attempting to prepare a bibliography of diabetes education materials for adults with limited reading skills but hadn't been able to locate more than a handful of such materials. Their final bibliography, published in August 1979 after a considerable search, contained only twelve publications with a readability rating of grade 7 or below. Ten of these twelve were from two sets of single-concept pamphlets, including those prepared by our RMP project. The remainder of the bibliography contained only another seven items with a readability rating of grade 8 or 9. Thus even with myriads of printed teaching materials on diabetes available, only a very few were appropriate for the large patient population with poor or even intermediate reading skills.

As the wide gap between the readability level of commonly used health-teaching materials and patients' reading comprehension skills became defined, the authors of *Teaching Patients With Low Literacy Skills* started holding workshops for health professionals, presenting some of the theory and how-to's for teaching poor readers. Feedback from the workshops was always extremely positive, and I have personally seen many changes in practice as a result. The content of the workshops has now been incorporated in this book, and I hail it as filling a large void in the teaching tools and methodologies readily available to health professionals. Not only can it help increase awareness of the specific problem, but it can also serve as a valuable reference in planning health teaching strategies for poor readers.

Patricia A. Lawrence, R.N., M.A.
Associate Professor
School of Nursing
University of North Carolina at
Chapel Hill
Chapel Hill, North Carolina

PREFACE

Teaching Patients With Low Literacy Skills comes from the combined experiences of three people who have one common concern—an awareness of the confusion and pain that accompany an inability to read. Each of the three has tried to alleviate that pain in some way. Len and Ceci Doak (husband and wife) have been volunteer tutors to nonreading adults. Jane Root has been a principal designer of tutor training materials used by Literacy Volunteers of America, an organization that trains and supports tutors nationwide. Jane and Len have both served as National President of that group.

Ceci Doak is retired from a lifetime of experience in the U.S. Public Health Service. She has worked worldwide as a public health educator. Len is a professional engineer with extensive experience in working with the Navy to reduce the reading level of technical manuals. Jane is Professor of Reading at Johnson State College, Vermont. She is a recognized authority and author in the field of reading.

Their combined talents and experience are merged in this book with the hope that it will be useful to all who teach patients directly as well as to teachers of health care providers. In-service program planners, nursing school instructors, medical school patient communication classes, community college nursing instructors, dietitians, physicians, therapists, and health educators will find this book a valuable help in working more effectively with patients.

When we first began to talk about the problems poor readers have in obtaining and understanding health information, we realized that an answer might lie in a multi-discipline approach using health education, linguistics, literacy research, and the practical lessons learned from volunteer agencies.

We were already aware of the reading problems of a large group of our fellow Americans. What we didn't know was how they coped with health instructions they could not understand. How do they handle the printed instructions for hospital rules and procedures? The medication instructions? The host of other materials? We supposed they faked it, or asked a friend to help, or perhaps only partly understood it, or ignored the instruction completely and hoped for the best. Could something be done to relieve this situation? We decided to try.

First we had to define the extent of the problem. For this we researched the literature and drew upon our collective experience. We evaluated hundreds of instructional materials and tested the reading skills of patients in hospital and clinic settings. We found, as we had expected, that there is a huge mismatch between the reading skills of the patients and the reading levels demanded by the instructions. We interviewed health care providers and observed patient instruction in hospitals and clinics. We developed approaches to reducing the literacy demand of health instructions and to improving patient understanding. Armed with this information, we prepared professional papers and conducted workshops for health care providers. Increasingly, it became evident that a text was needed to give the widest possible audience a chance to deal with the issue. This book is the result of our efforts to meet this need.

As you read, you will learn about the extent of the problem and the many ways in which poor reading can affect skills for coping with life including those that are health related. You will learn about ways to test the levels of patient comprehension and you will be asked to consider many techniques that will improve the levels of patient under-standing. We offer teaching strategies that should make your job easier, whether you are teaching with text, visuals, or audio tapes.

As much as possible, we have endeavored to make each chapter a complete unit of information, reducing the necessity of referring frequently to other chapters. The book is intended as a manual or "cookbook" to help instructors use text, tapes, and visuals more effectively with patients with limited literacy skills. The book provides strategies for teaching patients and techniques for evaluating instructions.

While we wait for someone to solve the problem of using "he" or "she" as an indefinite pronoun, we are equivocating. We usually rely on the traditional solution of using "he" to refer generally to either sex. This approach is not entirely satisfactory, but it seems to be the best we can do.

We have tried to make our suggestions practical. Indeed we have practiced what we preach. We have written simplified materials, we have tested hospital populations for comprehension, and we have worked at simplifying the process of health instruction. But we all have much to learn and much to share. We welcome your suggestions. We know that we face a future where education will play an increasing role in health maintenance. If we are to improve the chances of health for all people, those who are vulnerable because of poor reading skills must receive our concern. We offer this book as a place to start.

Cecilia Conrath Doak, M.P.H.
Leonard G. Doak, B.S., P.E.
Jane H. Root, Ph.D.

ACKNOWLEDGMENTS

We would like to express our sincere gratitude to the reviewers of our manuscript, all of whom are authorities in their specialities, for their contribution. The levels of expertise and experience represented would be impossible for one individual to duplicate. Their lively discussion of the content brought to light imperfections that served to reinforce our belief in the value of "pretesting." Each of them are to be commended for their excellent comments.

They are

Darryll J. Candy, M.B., B.S. (London)
Director, Primary Health Care
Catholic Health Service
Yaoundé, Cameroon

Claire Forbes, R.D.
Chief, Nutrition Services
Chronic Disease Control
Maryland Department of Health and Mental Hygiene
Baltimore, Maryland

Dorothy Gohdes, M.D.
Program Director
Indian Health Service Diabetes Project
Albuquerque, New Mexico

Keatha K. Krueger, Ph.D.
Diabetes Centers Program Director
Division of Diabetes, Endocrinology, and Metabolic Diseases
National Institute of Arthritis, Diabetes, and
    Digestive and Kidney Diseases
National Institutes of Health
Bethesda, Maryland

Patricia Lawrence, R.N., M.A.
Associate Professor
School of Nursing
University of North Carolina at Chapel Hill
Chapel Hill, North Carolina

Christine Ling, M.P.H.
Chief, Health Promotion and Education Office
Department of Health
State of Hawaii
Honolulu, Hawaii

Lois F. Lipsett, Ph.D.
Chief, Special Programs Branch
Division of Diabetes, Endocrinology, and Metabolic Diseases
National Institute of Arthritis, Diabetes, and Digestive and
    Kidney Diseases
National Institutes of Health
Bethesda, Maryland

Clarence E. Pearson, M.P.H.
Assistant Vice-President
Health and Safety Education Division
Metropolitan Life Insurance Company
New York, New York

Jeannette Simmons, D.Sc.
Clinical Professor
Department of Community and Family Medicine
Dartmouth Medical School
Hanover, New Hampshire

CONTENTS

CHAPTER ONE

The Problem

Twenty-three million American adults may not be able to comprehend what health professionals are talking about. They probably don't understand written instructions, audiovisual aids, or even tape recordings. These adults have been labeled as functionally illiterate. Although they wear no visible labels and have no visible signs of disability, they are found everywhere. They may be poor or affluent, and they may have almost any level of schooling. In addition, there is a large and rapidly growing elderly population with various kinds of learning impairments and a sizable group of people with learning disabilities.

The purpose of this book is to help health professionals get their messages across to this large segment of the patient population.

MAGNITUDE OF THE LITERACY PROBLEM

Northcutt's national study, Adult Performance Level (Roth, 1976), showed that 19.8% of the adult American population, or one out of every five American adults, lacks the literacy skills needed to function effectively in today's society.* This is generally interpreted as having reading skills below the fifth-grade level.

The study, which involved four years of surveying and testing more than 10,000 people, showed that these adults cannot use reference documents or catalogs effectively or follow instruction sheets. Some of these adults are not aware that the average body temperature is 98.6° Fahrenheit. They

*What is equally disturbing is that another 33.9% of the population is only marginally competent.

cannot address an envelope properly, read a menu to order food in a restaurant, or comprehend a simple road map, much less a graph or a bar chart.

Let's consider these handicaps in the context of our high-tech society. New technology, new products, and more complicated functions to perform raise the basic language skills required for survival. More and more people are falling behind by not being able to keep pace with the increased demands of our sophisticated culture.

For instance, a sixth-grade reading level is required to understand a driver's license manual. If you want to eat a frozen TV dinner, you need an eighth-grade reading level to follow the instructions. And you need a tenth-grade reading level to follow the instructions on a bottle of aspirin.

IMPACT ON HEALTH

Like all people, people with low literacy skills get sick, go to doctors, or attend clinics, and sometimes are hospitalized; most of all, like the rest of us, they want to prevent complications. The challenge we face in patient education is coping with this large number of people whose reading, writing, listening, and speaking skills are not well developed. Our job is to see how we can work around this barrier so that these patients will be able to carry out at least a minimum set of instructions in an effective manner.

Let's look briefly at the reading level of a number of health instructions. In 1979, we assessed the match between the literacy requirements of health instructions and the literacy abilities of patients. These studies were undertaken at the United States Public Health Service Hospital in Norfolk, Virginia (Doak and Doak, 1980).

In the Norfolk study we collected 100 examples of patient education materials, ranging from the Patient's Bill of Rights to the most explicit diet instructions. The mean reading level required to understand these materials was at the tenth-grade level. We then evaluated the reading ability of patients. Although the patients usually stated that they were high-school graduates, on the average they had word-recognition skills at about the seventh-grade level. This study was later replicated by the Diabetes Control Project, South Carolina Department of

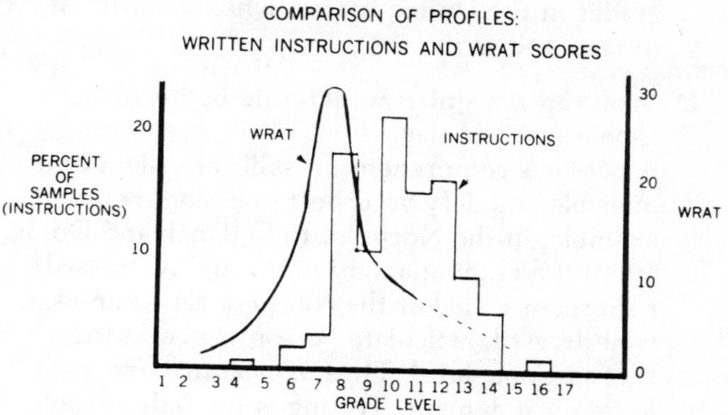

COMPARISON OF PROFILES:
WRITTEN INSTRUCTIONS AND WRAT SCORES

FIG. 1-1. *Patient word-recognition levels. Wide Range Achievement Test (WRAT) compared with levels of educational materials used with patients. (Doak LG, Doak CC: Patient comprehension profiles: Recent findings and strategies. Patient Counselling and Health Education 2, No. 3: 104, Winter, 1980. Reprinted with permission.)*

Health and Environmental Control, 1980–1981 (McNeal et al, 1984). The findings from this second study correlated with ours.

From Figure 1-1, it is clear that there is a gross mismatch between the level of difficulty of the materials and the word-recognition ability of the patients.

MYTHS ABOUT ILLITERACY

A number of common but false assumptions about illiteracy need to be addressed before we proceed. Let's take a look at some of these myths or assumptions:

☐ "Illiterates are dumb and learn slowly, if at all"—**False**
Throughout the entire world today nearly 800 million people are illiterate (Boyer, 1978), so lack of reading ability is not a mark of pathology. Even in the United States, many low-literacy people have average IQs and can speak articulately. However, for one reason or another they did not learn to read during that narrow window in time, usually in the second and third

grades in the United States, when we are taught to read and write.

☐ "You can recognize an illiterate by his or her appearance"—**False**
A person's comprehension skills are silent and invisible and defy your best guessing. For example, in the Norfolk Study (Doak and Doak, 1980) the reading ability of a roughly dressed fisherman tested at the college level whereas a well-dressed, articulate person tested at the second-grade level. Thus, appearance is a poor basis for judgment. Testing is the only reliable way of determining a person's literacy skills.

☐ "Years of schooling completed correlates well with the person's literacy level"—**False**
The years of schooling completed tells you what the person has been exposed to, not what his or her language and comprehension skill level is today. In the Norfolk Study (1980) most patients declared that they had completed high school; however, they are functioning today at the seventh-grade level even in the simplest reading skill—recognizing words.

☐ "Most illiterates are foreigners or poor, black, and from the South"—**False**
Illiteracy is found in every walk of life, among all races, and at all socioeconomic strata. Although it is true that foreigners, poor people, and blacks may have a greater number of school drop-outs, the literacy problem cannot be defined along racial or socioeconomic lines.

☐ "Most illiterates will tell you if they don't understand"—**False**
They will almost always seek to conceal the fact that they cannot read or do not understand. There is a strong social stigma attached to illiteracy. To avoid discovery when confronted with a reading situation, most will use excuses such as "I forgot my glasses"; "I want my husband (or wife) to see this first"; or "Would you read this for me? My eyes are tired."

SOURCES OF MYTHS
ABOUT ILLITERACY

Many myths or false assumptions arise from the way a person talks. If the person says "dem" and "dose" for "them" and "those" or uses broken phrases or poor grammar such as "I done took watcha tole me to," we form a judgment about that person's intelligence (Shuy, 1976, 1977).

Not many of us understand that fluency and grammar are only **language** skills. Competency in the language process is not the only measure of intelligence. As a result of these stereotypes we may not make the effort to work at communication because we may think it is a losing game. Have you ever felt like "ho-hum" or "What's the use?" when faced with what seems an impossible challenge?

If you have the stereotype of the illiterate linked with limited learning capability, consider the highly developed memory skills in the following example of a young man tutored in a Literacy Volunteers of America program:

> John was 26 years old and held a good job as a machinist with a large manufacturer in a northeastern state. A reading test showed he read at less than a first-grade level. He could sign his name but he did not know many of the letters in his signature. He also knew enough arithmetic to figure his piecework sums. His employer did not know John was illiterate and had offered to promote him to foreman. John had to decline the promotion because he couldn't read the test required.
>
> When he was asked how he managed to read blueprints, a necessary part of his job, John replied, "When I get a new print, I take it home to my wife. She reads it to me and I memorize it. Then I go back the next day and make the part. It's a good thing we don't get new prints very often.

Such performance is evidence of high intellectual skill in the area of visual memory. This man was not stupid; he was simply nonfunctional in reading.

LIMITATIONS OF PATIENTS WITH
LOW LITERACY SKILLS

The limitations of patients with low literacy skills may be in the organization of perception or thought or in the disabilities of vocabulary and language. Briefly, comprehension is a highly complex process with logic, language, and experience all working together (Colvin and Root, 1976). The brain processes information at unbelievably fast rates of speed. This processing involves a tremendous storage capacity from which we transform symbols and images into knowledge. Logic, language, and experience all operate interdependently in the comprehension process, but this processing for the poor reader is much slower and less complete than for the competent reader.

For example, many patients do not have fluency with the letters in the alphabet and therefore must read each letter in a word in order to recognize the word. They often read one word at a time in a halting fashion. They may be able to make out typewritten material or small printed letters like these on this page, but they may not read as well if the message is in CAPITAL letters or in *handwriting*.

Reading is a key source of data for literate persons, but those who can't read must operate on a much more restricted information base. For example, in testing a group of 28 adults enrolled in a basic reading course in Washington, D.C., we found all could recognize the words "go" and "stop," but none could read a traffic sign that said "Merging Traffic," "Yield," or "Thruway." They had no idea what those signs said nor what driving behavior was expected from them.

Abbreviations, even such simple ones as those for the days of the week or the months of the year, are a real problem. Patients may not be able to "read" a clock to tell the time of day. Many cannot read appointment slips, especially if the time and date information is handwritten.

Patients may have limited vocabulary even for relatively common words used for instruction purposes. These words slow down the decoding process in the memory system. For instance, a film on exercise for people with arthritis may use language considered relatively simple, but as soon as the script talks about "alternating" arms, "forearm" resting "firmly," and "quad sets," or later gets into "isometric," "gluteal sets," or "resistive and positioning" exercises, these patients with low literacy skills have not only slowed down, they've dropped out!

Most of these people have learned to respond to this kind of situation and have had lots of experience in dealing with people who are impatient or frustrated with them. One of the ways they cope is to agree with whatever is asked of them. Thus, if you ask them, "Do you understand?" they answer "Yes." If they had answered "No," they would have been called on to explain what they didn't know, and they may not have the vocabulary or fluency to explain what they did not understand.

Poor readers and persons who cannot read at all usually do not ask questions to obtain information. This is partly because asking questions requires a level of problem-solving skills they may not have developed, partly because they have a poor vocabulary, and partly because their questions were brushed off in the past as irrelevant or incoherent.

There is a body of knowledge from the literature and research in sociology that addresses the problems of those with poor communication skills. A summary of these findings is presented below to provide the reader with an insight to these important data (Schatzman and Strauss, 1955).

☐ **A patient's perspective tends to be limited to direct personal experience.**
  Interpretation: Descriptions of events or information of any kind is perceived only through its meaning to the patient. Relationships to other people or to other times are seldom perceived.
  Example: The patient's response to information about the risk of people getting the flu was, "I didn't listen to you. I got my flu booster. None of that stuff I need."

☐ **A patient may be insensitive to the need to give information to health-care providers.**
  Interpretation: The tendency is for the patient to take for granted that others understand the same way as he does. Therefore there is no need to clarify or explain events.
  Example: One patient's response to questions during a medical history was, "If he has to ask a lot of questions, he can't be a very good doctor."

☐ **A patient does not think in terms of classes of information or of categories.**
  Interpretation: Thinking is mainly in specific, concrete terms for poor readers. Not accustomed to handling a volume of data, the person with

low literacy skills doesn't see the need for indexing, groupings, or lists.

Example: The grouping of foods in a diet plan into categories of proteins, cereals, fats, and so forth is confusing to the point of the poor reader ignoring the whole message.

☐ **A patient gives information in bits and pieces without an identifiable pattern.**

Interpretation: One statement becomes the trigger for another without a logical connection from one statement to the next. Valuable data can come from this digression, but it is often difficult to place the information in context.

Example: When asked about foot care, one patient responded with a long garbled account of his surgical experience. All the instructor wanted to know was if the patient knew how to cut his toenails correctly.

Confusion arises in many different ways because of differences in the organization of thought and perception and a limited vocabulary. The consequences can be minor or major. For instance, the following account by a patient shows how minor inconvenience occurred because the patient could not read a sign:

I had to go to the clinic for x-rays. The girl at the desk told me which room to go to and I went in and sat down. Quite a few other people came in. Pretty soon I saw that those who came after me were being called, but I never was. I sat there for almost an hour before I finally asked the nurse when my turn was. She asked if I had signed the register. When I said "No," she pointed to the sign in front of her desk that said "Please sign the register when you come in." I didn't tell her I couldn't read. She took me next. (Personal Communication: Literacy Volunteers of America, Inc., Syracuse, NY, 1980)

Sometimes the situation is much more serious and can even result in death. One physician illustrated this point by citing his experience:

A baby was brought to the hospital with diarrhea. I treated the baby and told the mother to "push fluids"

with the baby. This was at 8:00 A.M. The mother took
the baby home and at noon the baby was dead. The
mother had literally pushed fluids by tipping the baby's
bottle upside down and forcing the fluids when the
baby's response began to slow down. The baby
suffocated. (McKeever et al, 1958)

To the patient who is eager to follow instructions, the
literal meaning may be the only message that comes across. In
the example above, the nuances of the action required of the
mother, such as allowing the baby time to swallow, breathe, or
relax, or for burping the baby, all of these steps of the feeding
process are lost in the force of the verb "push."

Highly literate people use a wide range of adjectives and
examples that provide variety as well as reduce ambiguity in
their written and oral communications. The less literate person
does not have this fluency so word variety may cause accuracy
to suffer and comprehension to be reduced when used in
instructions. For instance, the highly literate person may
describe pain as dull or sharp; episodic or continuous; related to
time of day, eating, or body activity; or limited to a particular
area. But the less literate person may be able to say only, "I hurt
here."

People with low literacy skills have not developed their
comprehension skills for analyzing instructions or for synthe-
sizing information to make it fit into a behavior nor have they
acquired the problem-solving skills of drawing inferences and
conclusions from experience. These are their big limitations.

THE OUTLOOK

What does all this mean for those of us who are involved in
providing health care? It means that changes must be made in
the content, the presentation process, and the literacy demand
of health-care instructions if patients are to achieve a reasonable
level of competency for the self-management of their health
problems.

Self-help can never become a reality for people with low
literacy skills in our society unless they can comprehend what
they are supposed to do. The objective of this book is to provide
teaching strategies to help make self-help and self-management
a reality.

Teaching strategies need to change to meet the levels of logic, language, and experience of these patients. The changes we suggest are more of an adaptation of existing methods rather than the development of new ones. These changes are built on knowledge, research, and experience from the fields of reading, literacy, and health education. These changes offer enormous payoffs in better patient comprehension of health information and thereby raise the possibility of better patient compliance.

REFERENCES

Boyer EL (U.S. Commissioner of Education): A commitment to literacy. Address given at the International Literacy Conference. Washington, DC, September 8, 1978

Colvin RJ, Root JH: Tutor: Techniques Used in the Teaching of Reading, rev. ed, pp 47–50. Syracuse, NY, Literacy Volunteers of America, Inc., 1976

Doak LG, Doak CC: Patient comprehension profiles: Recent findings and strategies. Patient Counselling and Health Education 2, No. 3:101–106, 1980

McNeal B, et al: Comprehension Assessment of Diabetes Education Program Participants. South Carolina Diabetes Control Project, South Carolina. Department of Health and Environment, Control, p. 33, Columbia, SC. Diabetes Care, May/June, 1984

Roth E: APL: A ferment in education. American Education 12, No. 4:6–9, May, 1976

Schatzman L, Strauss A: Social class and modes of communication. American Journal of Sociology LX, No. 4:329–338, January, 1955

Shuy RW: How misconceptions about language affect judgments about intelligence. Papers in Applied Linguistics, Linguistics and Reading, Series 1, pp 1–9. Arlington, VA, Center for Applied Linguistics, April 1977

Shuy RW: The medical interview: Problems in communication. Primary Care 3, No. 3: 365–386, September, 1976

McKeever N, Skinner ML, Conrath C: Stimulating Improved Health Practices Among Selected Indian Groups. Public Health Service, Bureau of Indian Health, December, 1958 (unpublished)

CHAPTER TWO

Theories of Comprehension: The State of the Art

It is easy to believe that a patient can learn if he really wants to. The assumption is that all you have to do is present the information to the patient. The conclusion is that comprehension will occur when information is given. But information delivery is on your side of the equation, whereas comprehension is controlled by the patient. Simply receiving the message has little correlation with understanding the message. (Tuman, 1980).

Comprehension is a complex process that depends on the effective interaction of logic, language, and experience, as well as other factors. Comprehension results in **grasping the meaning** of the instruction.

To help make this chapter more meaningful for your work, we suggest that you review a piece of instructional material you are currently using and relate it to the topics covered in this chapter as you read along. Almost any instructional material will do as an example.

Think about the instructions and the messages that you want to deliver to your patients.

Do you have a piece in mind now? . . . Let's walk through the process as your patient experiences the reading and thinking that you hope will ultimately result in comprehending the messages contained in the pamphlet. Using this frame of reference, we hope the information we wish to share with you will become clear.

PURPOSE OF THE MATERIAL

All of us read for some reason or another. Sometimes we read to obtain specific information, to identify facts, or to help us remember a message. Sometimes we want to evaluate data, to gain an overview of procedures, or to use information to help us make choices. These are all purposes for reading.

Now, about the example of instructional material that you have in mind. Can you quickly identify the reason you want the patient to read it? Let's suppose it is intended to deliver specific information so the patient can make a decision.

HOW MATERIAL IS LEARNED

Readiness to Learn

Telling the patient why you want him to read the pamphlet may help overcome the hurdle of patient motivation and interest. Removing these hurdles is essential in the comprehension process.

You can go a step further here. If you open the pamphlet to the page where the specific information is presented and point out the paragraphs you want the patient to understand, you will help him to develop an interest. Saying something like, "Let me show you the key points here," demonstrates your knowledge and your interest in the patient. Even if the patient doesn't read well, you can stimulate his readiness to understand.

Readiness on the part of the patient is critical for him to learn what you have to teach. You have something going for you when you make the effort to interest the patient because usually patients tend to respond positively to someone who wants to help them understand. The fact that they are in your clinical setting is at least a minimal acknowledgment that they want help, even though the actions they must take may be distasteful or even painful to them.

Many patients have spent a lifetime hiding their reading problem and getting by, so if you don't get much more than a nod and a half-hearted smile in response to your efforts, that's O.K. They've been called "dumb" and "stupid," so they realize how often low literacy is linked to low intelligence. It may be very difficult for them to take a chance that this stranger— you—who is so obviously competent will not think them stupid. Thus, even with you, they may try to fake it and muddle through if they can.

These first few minutes may be the most critical part of the learning experience. You need the patient's attention so that the memory system can swing into action.

The Initial Processing
of the Message

Let's return to the message that is in the instructional material you have in mind. That message has to start coming across to the patient **right now.** The patient must be able to perceive your message as relevant to him and as logical and do-able. That means that the language explaining the message must be understandable to him, and he has to be able to reorganize what he already knows to include your new message. That is a very tall order!

Why does all this have to happen so soon and at one time? It has to do with the way the memory systems in the brain function (Sticht et al, 1974). The first component in the brain's memory system, the sensory information system, receives the printed (or spoken) words, pictures, or demonstrations. The transmission of these images or symbols is very rapid, on the order of 300 milliseconds per image. The brain's storage capacity is very large, but the storage time is very short because its function is only to display information for recoding in a different form if the person wants to keep the information. As you can imagine, many images are lost before they are processed because processing is done only one image at a time.

What determines that some images are processed and others are not? This is a very important point. The mind must **actively** direct attention to the image and give it a priority. Do I like this message? Do I want it? Do I understand it?

Let's say that the patient likes your message, understands it, and wants to remember it. Now what happens?

The Beginning Stage of
Remembering the Message

The short-term memory, "scratch pad" or "working memory," handles the critical beginning stages of remembering. The most recent research indicates that when a person is paying attention to what he's seeing or hearing, electrical wave patterns can be detected within several centers of the brain that are responsible for processing different kinds of information (Jonassen, 1982).

For instance, visual material in photographic form is processed in one brain center; written text in another; numbers in another; muscular movement, such as writing notes or muscular processing if you are having the patient interact with equipment, occupies another brain area. Each of these types of information involves electrical activity in a separate center of the brain.

That's not all. As the patient starts to interact with your instructional material, chemical changes must occur in the brain for long-term storage. Proteins present in membranes of cells start a chain reaction by activating large numbers of neurons, which in turn activate storage sites in the brain. The storage sites are critical if you want the patient to remember your message, but unless your message is committed to these storage sites in long-term memory, it is lost. The proteins just mentioned have a very short life span and are soon destroyed. When they are destroyed, the short-term electrical memory can be cleared for a new set of signals. The effect is similar to pressing the "clear" button on a calculator.

Short-term storage lasts from one-fourth of a second to a maximum of one hour. If you rehearse the material and go over it again and again, you can extend the time, but usually not beyond eight hours (Jonassen, 1982.) So short-term storage is indeed temporary. The storage capacity is very small. For average adults about five to seven unrelated items can be retained at one time. Unless the items can be hooked up with already known information, in a process called "chunking," the items are destroyed and the message is gone.

The more you can help the patient at this stage, for example, by using words he already knows and in a context that he's familiar with, the better he can keep up with you and begin to process the flow of information into long-term memory.

Let's try this point out: we're going to give you a list of words and we want you to read the list once as if you were listening to us read it to you. When you finish reading both columns of the list, close this book and repeat the whole list out loud, just the way it was presented to you:

the	and
on	steam
stove	fresh
green	pan
will	the
in	a
yellow	vegetables

Could you repeat the list? Did you have any trouble remembering 14 items? Let's rearrange the list into a meaningful context like this: "The fresh green and yellow vegetables will steam in a pan on the stove." Now the words make sense, and you can remember such a sentence much more readily than you can remember disconnected words. This is called chunking. It is the placement of words in a meaningful context to facilitate remembering the message.

How does chunking work in patient education materials? Suppose you give a patient a diabetes manual to read. He turns to the section on diet and finds this sentence:

> Alcoholic ingestion superimposed upon inadequate dietary intake can precipitate acute hypoglycemia. (Diet in the Treatment of Hypoglycemia, 1977)

If the patient can read the sentence at all, he reads it word by word rather than by scanning, so the reading is tedious and tiring. Undoubtedly he doesn't understand the words. Since he doesn't understand the words, he can't go through the process of "chunking" with what he already knows. Suppose the sentence in the manual had been written in simpler language:

> Do not drink beer, wine, or booze on an empty stomach.

The simpler message would have provided some recommended action and the patient would know what he was supposed to do. The words would have been familiar to him, and the message would be one he could understand.

Let's return now to the instructional material you have in mind. Are the words, pictures, or illustrations likely to be familiar to your patients? What we have said so far is that the patient has to perceive the facts the way you intend, and he must be able to associate the new data with what he already knows. Each message enters the field of consciousness through printed or spoken words or through pictures or demonstrations. Each word, picture, or demonstration must link up with a reservoir of similar ones stored in the brain so that they build up to a coherent and understandable whole. Small gaps in this building process can be overcome if most of the symbols and building blocks are familiar. But if a number of the critical words and ideas are uncertain or totally new, the building process falls apart and the message self-destructs.

Building a New Frame of Reference

Suppose the concepts you have to teach are likely to be unknown or unfamiliar to your patients. In order to achieve strong patient understanding and reliable compliance, you may need to teach some new terms or reorganize some existing ideas. New information must be presented in small repetitive steps.

New ideas can be linked with already known information through analogies, examples, case studies, drawings, or pictures. You may prefer to model by demonstrating a step-by-step procedure.

To achieve full understanding for **long-term memory** it is usually necessary to do two things:

1. To have more than one encounter with the parts and the whole of a new idea
2. To arrange for the learner to talk about and demonstrate the new ideas and procedures

When the patient demonstrates or explains the instruction given, the feedback thus supplied is an essential evaluation of instruction. If the patient can convert the instruction into a different form, as, for example, by saying it in his own words or demonstrating it, then comprehension has occurred, at least for the short-term.

INTERFERENCES TO LEARNING

This is an appropriate time to point out one source of trouble in teaching new concepts: the problem of masking. Masking occurs when a word in your instruction has a different meaning from the one understood by the patient. The following is an example of masking:

> The discharge nurse said to the new mother, "Now you know to watch the baby's stools to be sure they're normal . . . you do know what normal stools look like, don't you?"
>
> To which the mother replied, "Oh, yeah, sure . . . I've got four of them in my kitchen."

Another example of masking occurs in diet instruction with the word "servings." The amount of a serving varies from one type of food to another. These differences have to be stressed in teaching so that the patient can store them in separate categories or subcategories (Jonassen, 1982).

There are other kinds of interference that affect the comprehension of new material, one of which is anxiety. For example, anxiety could occur if the patient knows that an important encounter with the physician is just ahead.

Drugs can be another source of interference. Drugs meant to lessen pain can also depress the patient's attention and his word processing and therefore his ability to learn. Without drugs, however, discomfort can crowd out all other stimuli, and especially an intellectual and complex message. If you must instruct under these conditions, be aware that the patient's comprehension may be seriously hampered. If possible, plans should be made at this time for instruction at a later date.

SUMMARY

Your goal is for the patient to process your message and to decide to make a permanent behavior change. To do this, your message must get through the maze of short-term memory into the long-term storage.

Much of the rest of this book is devoted to ways you can improve your message delivery so that behavior change is more likely for adults with low literacy skills.

Remember that three factors interact to support comprehension: logic, language, and experience. Patients must see that what you suggest makes sense, fits within their current lifestyles, can be achieved, and is worthwhile to pursue. They must find that the language you use to explain your point is close to their own vernacular so they encounter few stumbling blocks in learning.

Patients must have personal experience similar enough to what you suggest so that they can put it all together in their imaginations while they are with you and so that your message can be translated into overt behavior at some other time when you are not there. If you encounter comprehension difficulties, look for the reasons in one or more of these three areas: logic, language, and experience.

REFERENCES

Diet in the Treatment of Hypoglycemia. U.S. Public Health Service Hospital, Norfolk, VA. PHSH (NOR) 247, August, 1977

Jonassen DH: The Technology of Text: Principles for Structuring, Designing, and Displaying Text, pp 91–119. Englewood Cliffs, NJ, Educational Technology Publications, 1982

Sticht TG, et al: Auding and Reading: A Developmental Model, pp 48–50. Alexandria, VA, Human Resources Research Organization (HumRRO), 1974

Tuman MC: A comparative review of reading and listening comprehension. Journal of Reading 23, No. 8:702, May, 1980

CHAPTER THREE

Testing Patient Comprehension

Testing the ability of patients to comprehend is a relatively new concept in the health field. In the field of education, however, the procedures are used routinely. There are dozens of standardized tests that provide valid and reliable information.

In the health-care system, instructional testing is usually limited to written pre- and post-tests that measure recall of knowledge rather than comprehension. Thus, information about how well or poorly a patient may understand is seldom obtained. If you are to teach patients, data about their comprehension abilities must be determined so that the patients understand as fully as possible.

Finding out which of your patients can read and understand your materials may be measured directly, and in this chapter we will suggest testing methods. Indirect methods to assess the appropriateness of instructional materials are also presented. One such method is to allow patients to choose from among a variety of ways to learn, each of which requires a different level of literacy.

Let's begin with a direct way to assess comprehension—the cloze technique (McKenna, 1980). This technique has the advantage of giving you an objective measure of a patient's ability to read and to comprehend written information.

THE CLOZE TECHNIQUE

Description

Developed by Taylor (1953), the cloze* procedure measures a person's ability to comprehend a written passage. The test is systematically designed so that every fifth word is deleted

*Cloze is derived from the word "closure."

19

from a passage, and the reader's task is to determine the missing words and to fill in the blanks. This requires that the reader be sensitive to grammatical, syntactical, and semantic clues. The ability of people to supply the missing words is a significant indicator of how well they comprehend the material.

The cloze technique tests the comprehension process in two ways: (1) it tests how much knowledge was obtained from the text surrounding the blank and (2) determines how well this information was used to obtain additional information (Bormuth, 1975).

Packaged cloze tests are widely used in school systems, and these tests are available from commercial sources. However, we recommend that you make up your own tests because the results will show the patient's comprehension level of **your** instructions. Your test results will then show which words or sentences present the greatest comprehension problem for your patients. The problem words or sentences can then be revised to make them easier to understand.

Constructing a Cloze Test

1. Select a prose passage from instructional material you are now using. Pamphlets, brochures, instruction sheets, and manuals are all useful for this purpose. Be sure the passage consists of prose without reference to figures, tables, charts, or pictures.

   Choose material not previously read by your patients but that is typical of the instructions you are giving. The material should include complete paragraphs so that the readers will have the benefit of complete thought units.

2. Leaving the first and last sentences intact, delete every fifth word for a total of about 50 deleted words. Do not delete proper nouns (delete the word following the proper noun). Replace all deleted words with a line, or blank. All blanks should be of equal length (see Sample Cloze Test).

Sample Cloze Test—Control Chronic Obstructive Pulmonary Disease (COPD)

Medications

The pharmacist will explain the correct way to take the medications that your doctor has prescribed for you.

Do not take any _____ or cold remedies, including _____ you buy without a _____, without first checking with _____ doctor. These medications can _____ it more difficult for _____ to cough up the _____ from your lungs. If _____ sputum is not removed _____ your lungs, you can _____ get a respiratory or _____ infection.

Remember, mixing medications, _____ those that can be _____ without a prescription, can _____ dangerous. If you are _____ medications that have been _____ for other reasons, be _____ to inform your doctor.

Coughing

"Pursed lip breathing" is _____ way to help remove _____ air in your lungs. _____ is done by inhaling _____ your nose with your _____ closed, exhaling through your _____ with your lips pursed _____ as in a kissing _____ whistling position and making _____ (breathing out) twice as _____ as for inhalation.

Postural _____ is a method of _____ gravity and chest percussion _____ loosen and help remove _____ from your lungs. This _____ done by lying in _____ positions with someone properly _____ your lung area with _____ hands. The physical therapist _____ show you how this _____ done.

It is important _____ you drink plenty of _____, especially water. The water _____ the sputum in your _____ and makes it easier _____ cough. You can increase _____ in your diet with _____, Jell-O, or even Popsicles.

(*continued*)

Sample Cloze Test (*continued*)

_____ your doctor how much _____ he wants you to _____ each day. It will _____ if you eat smaller _____ frequent meals because large _____ make it harder to breathe. If you become short of breath while eating, take a short rest period before and after meals.

(*Control C.O.P.D.*, Hampton General Hospital, 3120 Victoria Boulevard, Hampton, VA 23669)

Giving a Cloze Test

It's best to be honest about the purpose behind asking a patient to do a "cloze" activity. You may start with a statement such as, "To help you be **well**, it's my job to see that you have directions and instructions that are right for you. If these are not right, it's my job to get you some that are. It's important for you to really understand what you are to do, and we certainly don't want poor directions to get in your way."

Most patients want to help and are willing to participate in this kind of testing activity. In the Norfolk study, we had only 6 patients out of a sample of 100 who chose not to participate (Doak and Doak, 1980).

If the patient seems totally confused or is reluctant to participate, remove the material and say something like, "Well, that's not easy but there are other ways to manage this, so don't worry. It's my job to do the worrying on this one." Proceed to something else that is unlikely to be perceived as threatening by the patient.

Make the following points in your instructions to patients:

- ☐ Read through the entire test before attempting to fill in the blanks.
- ☐ Only one word should be written for each blank.
- ☐ Try to fill in every blank. It's O.K. to guess.
- ☐ Don't worry about your spelling. All I need to do is recognize the word.

This is not a timed test. If the patient is struggling, thank him for the effort and say something like, "Some of those are tricky to figure out, but don't worry. You don't have to do them all." Set the test aside and go on to something else. Do your scoring later.

Scoring the Cloze Test

1. Count as correct only those words that are exact replacements of the deleted words. Synonyms are **not** counted as correct. (You may bridle at the restriction against giving credit for synonyms. The possibility of a large number of synonyms has already been taken into account in the scoring criteria. That's why we use 60% exact replacements rather than 100% as evidence of full comprehension. By designating as acceptable only words that are exact replacements, you are freed from the need to determine the suitability of each and every possible alternative word. So count only **exact replacements.**)

2. Inappropriate word endings (-s, -ed, -er, -ing) should be counted as incorrect. Such mistakes usually indicate that the patient is not aware of the complete meaning of the sentence.

3. The raw score is the number of exact word replacements.

4. Divide the raw score by the total number of blanks to obtain the percentage of correct responses. If the passage has 50 blanks, for example, and if the patient had 30 correct responses, and 12 incorrect responses and left 8 blank, divide 30 by 50. The percentage in this case would be 60%.

5. For a score of 60% and above, consider the patient fully capable of understanding the material; for a score of 40% to 60%, consider the patient to be in need of supplemental instruction; for a score below 40%, consider the material as written to be too difficult for the patient.

To give you an idea of the variety of parts of speech needed for comprehension, here is the list of words deleted from the Sample Cloze Test:

1.	cough	26.	exhalation
2.	those	27.	long
3.	prescription	28.	drainage
4.	your	29.	using
5.	make	30.	to
6.	you	31.	secretions
7.	sputum	32.	is
8.	this	33.	certain
9.	from	34.	clapping
10.	easily	35.	cupped
11.	lung	36.	will
12.	even	37.	is
13.	bought	38.	that
14.	be	39.	fluids
15.	taking	40.	thins
16.	prescribed	41.	lungs
17.	sure	42.	to
18.	one	43.	fluids
19.	trapped	44.	soups
20.	This	45.	Ask
21.	through	46.	water
22.	mouth	47.	drink
23.	mouth	48.	help
24.	such	49.	more
25.	or	50.	meals

LISTENING TEST

Listening comprehension may well be much better than reading comprehension for your patient. However, don't count on it because this is not always the case. Here's a way to find out how much your patient understands or remembers when listening.

1. Select a passage from the materials you have chosen for instruction (see Sample Listening Test).

2. Say something like, "Some of us learn best when we hear things. Listen carefully, and when I am

finished I will ask you questions about what I have said."

3. Read the passage at a normal rate.
4. Ask 8 to 10 questions (see Sample Listening Test).
5. Find the percentage of correct answers by dividing the number right by the number possible. If the patient's score is about 75%, the material will be about right for instruction, but you may need to provide a little assistance for full comprehension. If the patient's score is 90%, the material will be easy for the patient and can be used independently (perhaps delivered by tape) with full comprehension. If the patient's score is less than 75%, this material will be too difficult for effective use and you will need to find or write simpler instructions. Test again at this lower level.

Sample Passages for Listening Test*

Shots

Most people see a doctor when they are sick. When you're sick it's easy to forget about the shots that could keep you from getting sick. Please listen to this and if you have any questions or need any of these shots, see your doctor.

The Flu

For a lot of people, the flu isn't a very bad illness, but some people get very sick with it and may even die from it. If you are one of these people who get very sick with it, you should have a flu shot every fall.

Talk to the doctor if you have not had a flu shot and if

1. You are 65 years old or older
2. You have diabetes or lung, heart, kidney, or liver trouble or another disease you've had for a long time

*Rewritten for lower reading level from the pamphlet *Flu and Pneumonia*, U.S. Public Health Service Hospital, Norfolk, VA, nd.

Pneumonia

There is a new shot against this disease. If you think you are one of the high-risk people who might get sick, ask your doctor about a shot. This might keep you from getting pneumonia.

Talk to your doctor if you have never had this shot and if

1. You have a disease you live with like lung, liver, kidney, or heart trouble, diabetes, alcoholism, or sickle cell anemia.

2. You have had your spleen taken out

Sample Questions for Listening Test

1. According to the information you've just heard, why do people not keep their shots up-to-date?
   Answer: They only see the doctor when they're sick.

2. What should you do if you think you need any of these shots?
   Answer: See your doctor.

3. How long does a flu shot protect you?
   Answer: About a year, or have a flu shot every fall.

4. What diseases make you more likely to need a flu shot?
   Answer: Diabetes, lung, heart, kidney, liver, or other chronic illness. (Any three would be a correct answer.)

5. At what age should older people have a flu shot?
   Answer: 65.

6. People have always died of pneumonia. Why is this disease less feared now?
   Answer: There is a new vaccine (shot) for pneumonia.

7. If you have an organ missing you should have a pneumonia shot. What organ is this?
   Answer: Spleen.

8. Some chronic diseases—those you learn to live with—also signal a need for pneumonia vaccine. What are they?
   Answer: Lung, liver, or kidney disease, heart trouble, diabetes, alcoholism, sickle cell anemia. (Any four would be a correct answer.)

WORD-RECOGNITION TEST

Most people equate the skill of reading with the ability to look at written words and transform them into oral language, or at least to understand enough of the words the author used to perceive the message intended. This is the rather mechanical, bottom-level skill of reading, but it is also a most necessary first step in comprehension. In a wider sense, this word-recognition aspect of reading is embedded in the logic, language, and experience needed by a reader to deal with the message in relation to his own purposes. If the patient can't read the words, comprehension never begins.

There are several tests available that could give you information about the reading skills of your patient. Most of them take 30 minutes or longer to administer, and that's likely to be too long for your purposes. One test, however, will give you an approximation of the functional reading level of an adult and will require only 5 minutes or so to administer. Although it surveys only one aspect of reading, word recognition, and leaves out vocabulary and comprehension, it is useful as a screening test. It is designed for people whose native language is English.

This test, which we will explain shortly, will indicate at what level the patient recognizes words. If the patient scores at the ninth- or tenth-grade level, a fair number of existing materials are likely to be satisfactory. If the patient scores at a lower-grade level, you will need to simplify those materials considerably or even use an entirely different instructional approach.

Description

The graded list of 100 words that serves as a screening test is the *Wide Range Achievement Test* (WRAT). A sample item from this test appears in Figure 3-1.

The patient is asked only to **pronounce** a list of words prepared from the scoring sheet illustrated in Figure 3-2. You prepare the word list from the score sheet. Place the words in columns.

The person administering the test listens carefully and scores the patient's responses on a master sheet (see Fig. 3-2), placing a pencil checkmark lightly above the word when it is

cat
see
red
to
big
work
book
eat
was
him

FIG. 3–1.   *Part of the list of words the patient reads for the word-recognition test. (Wide Range Achievement Test, p 4, Reading Level 1. Jastak Association, Inc. Copyright © 1978)*

WIDE RANGE

Page 4
Reading, Level I

Two letters in name (2)

cat   see   red   to

then   open   letter

weather   should   lip

approve   plot   huge

bulk   exhaust

recession   threshold

luxurious   rescinded

putative   endeavor

rudimentary   miscreant

seismograph   spurious

FIG. 3–2.   *Sample portion of score or master sheet. (Wide Range Achievement Test, p 4, Reading Level 1. Jastak Association, Inc. Copyright © 1978)*

Scoring Data From Right-Hand Side of WRAT Page

how	36
size	46
struck	56
urge	64
clarify	70
quarantine	76
repugnant	82
anomaly	88
mitosis	94
aborigines	100

Level I.
Raw Scores (RS)
and Grade Ratings (GR)

RS	GR	RS	GR
0	N.7	9	P.6
1	N.8	10	P.7
2	N.9	11	P.8
3	P.0	12	P.9
4	P.1	13	K.0
5	P.2	14	K.1
6	P.3	15	K.2
7	P.4	16	K.4
8	P.5	17	K.5

FIG. 3–3. *Sample portion of scoring data. (Wide Range Achievement Test. Jastak Association, Inc. Copyright © 1978)*

mispronounced. When three words are mispronounced, you stop the test. This means that the patient has usually reached his limit.

Scoring

The master sheet has the scoring for each line on the right-hand side of the page. You subtract the number of words the patient missed or didn't get to. This is the raw score (RS). Then look below at the table of raw scores to find the equivalent grade rating (GR) (Fig. 3-3).

Once you know the patient's approximate grade level for word recognition, you can use this information to select reading material that will match the patient's skill level. This approach to compatibility of reader and material is somewhat less conclusive than what can be done with the cloze technique, but it may be easier and less threatening to the patient and may therefore be preferred.

LITERACY SKILLS AS RELATED TO YEARS OF SCHOOLING

In the past, assumptions about a person's literacy skills were often made by equating reading competency with the last grade completed in school. The standard criterion for literacy used to be completion of the fifth grade. Recently, it has been customary not to fail children repeatedly for nonachievement but rather to relate grade placement to social needs as well as to academic progress. This has resulted in the promotion of some students to upper grades who lack reading skills that it is assumed they should have acquired in elementary school. The ideas of functional literacy have also replaced those of grade-level standards that were hard to measure and hard to define. The functional illiterate is a person who lacks the basic reading skills necessary to cope with the requirements of adult life.

Thus, "grades completed in school" is not a useful item of information on which to base assumptions about literacy. In the Norfolk Study, we found that most patients whose reading skills we assessed claimed to be high-school graduates (Doak and Doak, 1980). However, on a word-recognition test (WRAT) they scored about five grade levels below their stated twelfth-grade schooling. Either their achievement had always fallen short of their grade placement, or else the skills they once possessed had diminished through disuse.

COMPREHENSION RESTATEMENT

There are indirect ways to find out whether instructional material is appropriate for your patient. A very simple way to judge a patient's comprehension is to give standard instructional material to your patient. After the patient has read the material, ask for a restatement of the material in the patient's own words. A full and complete response will indicate satisfactory comprehension.

Lacking such a response, you can ask questions to determine if the patient has the relevant information. Lack of a full and ready response suggests inadequate comprehension even for **immediate** memory and is a signal that repetition or alternative instruction may be essential. This kind of questioning must be done on an individual basis; group questioning may not give you the information you need for specific patients.

PATIENT CHOICE OF INSTRUCTIONAL MEDIA

Perhaps the least threatening way to achieve a match between patient and information media is to make several different ways of learning available. In addition to printed material, you might prepare an audio tape to go along with a simplified text or as an alternative to text itself. (A full explanation on the production of audio tapes can be found in Chap. 7.) The tape may even have a related slide component or may direct the patient to the illustrations already available from printed sources.

When there is any doubt about patient literacy, you might say, "We've found that people learn in different ways, and they usually know which way works best for them. Some folks learn best by reading this pamphlet and others prefer to learn by listening. They seem to remember better when their eyes and their ears work together. So you go ahead and choose for yourself . . . either way, or both if you prefer. Here is the pamphlet, but the same information is available by listening to this tape. You may want to sit down here and try them out. You're free to listen more than once if you like . . . just press the yellow button to rewind the tape. When you think you have learned, I will want to talk with you to be sure you have fully understood. That's because you are in charge of maintaining your own health, but it is my job to see that you really know how. Let me know when you are finished."

When the patient has finished, or on your next visit to a hospitalized patient, say something like, "Now tell me what you know, and especially what you are to do." If the patient has poor recall, say, "That was a lot all at one time, I know. Let me go over a couple of things with you that are really important." Then re-teach, perhaps by demonstrating, by using food models, by referring to illstrations, or by using any way you can invent that gives some variety to the first approach; perhaps you could also reduce the amount of information provided.

When you think the patient has understood, again ask what he is to **do.** If more is needed, you might add, "Well, that's good and it's enough for now. There's more, but we'll work on that later. Thanks for your help."

This kind of approach may take a bit longer and may require more prepared material, but it may be one way to get directly to the task while still remaining aware of possible barriers to comprehension.

CONCLUSION

We encourage you to seriously consider finding out about your patients' comprehension abilities. We know from our workshops and testing experiences that many health-care providers feel hesitant about gathering data and inferring that a patient may have low literacy skills. There appears to be an implied personal inadequacy surrounding the failure to learn to read that does not seem to apply to physical problems such as kidney failure, unregulated metabolism, or inadequate sexual performance, even though these physical problems may be equally beyond the patient's immediate control.

Other than the Norfolk and South Carolina studies discussed in Chapter 1, there are few studies in the health literature on patient reading and comprehension. Mohammed (1964) reported that 77% of the patients studied in the Diabetes Clinic, University Hospitals, Cleveland, were unable to profit from written information being used at the time. An even earlier study by the National Tuberculosis Association (1958) showed little correlation between the level of education claimed by adults and actual reading ability. Larrabee (1977), who studied patient understanding of vocabulary terms used in initial health assessment, showed wide discrepancies in under-standing, similar to a much earlier work by Samora on medical vocabulary among hospital patients (1961). Much more work is reported in the literature on health beliefs, motivation, and perception than on comprehension.

Whichever way you choose—by measuring the match between patient and material by using the cloze technique or the WRAT reading score plus readability levels of materials, by testing patient comprehension of standard materials through questioning, or by offering patient choice of learning methods—

the goal is the same: to guarantee patient comprehension, which is a necessary prerequisite to the patient's compliance with medical instruction.

REFERENCES

Bormuth JR: The cloze procedure: Literacy in the classroom, pp 62–92. In Help for the Reading Teacher: New Directions for Research. National Conference on Research in English, Washington, DC, National Institute of Education (DHEW), March, 1975

Doak LG, Doak CC: Patient comprehension profiles: Recent findings and strategies. Patient Counselling and Health Education, 2, No. 3:103–104, Winter, 1980

Larrabee PD: Patients' Understanding of Vocabulary Terms Used in Initial Health Assessment. Dissertation, University of Rochester, 1977. University Microfilms International, 300 No. Zeeb Rd., Ann Arbor, MI 48106

McKenna, MC, Robinson RD: An Introduction to the Cloze Procedure: An Annotated Bibliography, rev ed. Newark, DE, International Reading Association, 1980

Mohammed M: Patients' understanding of written health information. Nursing Research 13:100–108, Spring, 1964

National Tuberculosis Association: Tuberculosis patients: How well they read and how much they know about tuberculosis. Focus, March, 1958

Samora J, et al: Medical vocabulary knowledge among hospital patients. Journal of Health and Human Behavior 2, No. 2:83–92, Summer, 1961

Taylor WS: Cloze procedure: A new test for measuring readability. Journalism Quarterly 30:415–433, Fall, 1953

Wide Range Achievement Test (WRAT): Jastak Association, Inc., 1526 Gilpin Ave., Wilmington, Delaware, 19806

CHAPTER FOUR

Testing Readability of Written Materials

There are more than 40 different formulas for assessing the degree of difficulty in reading materials. However, most of these formulas are quite similar in terms of the characteristics on which they focus. The most common characteristics are the **difficulty of the vocabulary** used and the **average sentence length.**

CHARACTERISTICS OF FORMULAS

Vocabulary difficulty is measured by the number of words in a passage of the material that do **not** appear on a standard list of "easy" words or by counting the number of multisyllabic words in the passage. Sentence length is measured by counting the average number of sentences in 100 running words. The choice of the formula used dictates the precise procedure to be followed and gives a result that may seem deceptively precise. At best, these formulas are approximations, measuring only the characteristics of the passage. They bypass the characteristics of the reader.

LIMITATIONS AND BENEFITS

Readers do not have equal competence in all materials even though the materials may have similar "readability levels" as measured by some formula. Readers' skills will vary with their interest and background of experience in a particular topic area. For example, a hypertensive patient who is already familiar with much of the vocabulary related to hypertension can read new material with much greater ease and under-standing than could a "new" hypertensive patient, although both might read other material with equal skill.

Despite such limitations, it is worth knowing how to assess readability of written material. This measure is a useful device when you have to make a decision between two pieces of material that vary in readability difficulty. It is also useful in helping you assess your own written materials and in checking your rewriting of material to achieve a lower reading level.

Readability is a valid and recognized research tool. It is also a useful tool when you want to present evidence concerning the problem of reading difficulty to a staff that may be skeptical of your data unless the data are substantiated by some established measure. For example, in the Norfolk Study, when hospital administrators learned that the surgical consent form tested at the 16th-grade level, immediate action was taken to reduce the level of reading difficulty of the form.

Out of the array of 40-plus possible established formulas to determine readability, we will present just two. We will also refer you to some of the many other formulas should you decide to explore this field further (Bormuth, 1966; Felker, 1980; Fry, 1977; McLaughlin, 1969; Rosenshine, 1969; Seels, 1971).

SMOG TESTING

The SMOG formula was originally developed by G. Harry McLaughlin in 1969. It will predict the grade-level difficulty of a passage within 1.5 grades in 68% of the passages tested. That may be close enough for your purposes. It is simple to use and faster than most other measures. The procedure is presented below.

Instructions

1. You will need 30 sentences. Count out 10 consecutive sentences near the beginning, 10 consecutive from the middle, and 10 from the end. For this purpose, a sentence is any string of words punctuated by a period (.), an exclamation point (!), or a question mark (?).

2. From the entire 30 sentences, count the words containing **three or more syllables,** including repetitions.
3. Obtain the grade level from Table 4-1, or you may calculate the grade level as follows: Determine the nearest perfect square root of the total number of words of three or more syllables and then add a constant of 3 to the square root to obtain the grade level.

Example:

Total number of multisyllabic (3 or more syllables) words	67
Nearest perfect square	64
Square root	8
Add constant of 3	11 This is the grade level.

Table 4-1.
SMOG Conversion Table

Word Count	Grade Level
0–2	4
3–6	5
7–12	6
13–20	7
21–30	8
31–42	9
43–56	10
57–72	11
73–90	12
91–110	13
111–132	14
133–156	15
157–182	16
183–210	17
211–240	18

Developed by: Harold C. McGraw, Office of Educational Research, Baltimore County Public Schools, Towson, Maryland.

Special Rules for SMOG Testing

☐ Hyphenated words are **one** word.

☐ For numerals, pronounce them aloud and count the syllables pronounced for each numeral (e.g., for the number 573, five = 1, hundred = 2, seventy = 3, and three = 1, or 7 syllables).

☐ Proper nouns should be counted.

☐ If a long sentence has a colon, consider each part of it as a separate sentence. However, if possible, avoid selecting that segment of the passage.

☐ The words for which the abbreviations stand should be read aloud to determine their syllable count (e.g., Oct. = October = 3 syllables).

SMOG on Shorter Passages

Sometimes it may be necessary to assess the readability of a passage of less than 30 sentences. You can still use the SMOG formula to obtain an approximate grade level by using a conversion number from Table 4-2 and then using Table 4-1 to find the grade level.

First count the number of sentences in your material and the number of words with three or more syllables. In Table 4-2, in the left-hand column, locate the number of sentences, and locate the conversion number in the column opposite. Multiply the word count found earlier by the conversion number. Use this number in Table 4-2 to obtain the corresponding grade level.

For example, suppose your material consisted of 15 sentences and you counted 12 words of three or more syllables in this material. Proceed as follows:

1. In Table 4-2, left-hand column, locate the number of sentences in your material. For your material, the number is 15.
2. Opposite 15 in the adjacent column, find the conversion number. The conversion number for 15 is 2.0.
3. Multiply your word count, 12, by 2 to get 24.
4. Now look at Table 4-1 to find the grade level. For a word count of 24, the grade level is 8.

Table 4–2.
**SMOG Conversion for Samples
With Fewer Than 30 Sentences**

Number of Sentences In Sample Material	Conversion Number
29	1.03
28	1.07
27	1.1
26	1.15
25	1.2
24	1.25
23	1.3
22	1.36
21	1.43
20	1.5
19	1.58
18	1.67
17	1.76
16	1.87
15	2.0
14	2.14
13	2.3
12	2.5
11	2.7
10	3

FRY READABILITY FORMULA

Dr. Edward Fry of Rutgers University developed another formula, which is relatively easy to use and is considered to be a valid and useful measure of readability (Fig. 4-1). It takes a few minutes longer than the SMOG formula, but it is considered to be a more accurate measure of readability. It may also be suitable for passages of less than 30 sentences (see Fig. 4-1 for the formula).

Either the SMOG or the Fry index of readability will help you determine the degree of difficulty in your reading materials. In combination with the WRAT reading test, a readability index

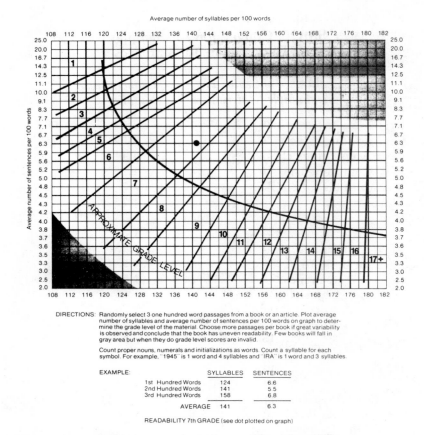

Average number of syllables per 100 words

DIRECTIONS: Randomly select 3 one hundred word passages from a book or an article. Plot average number of syllables and average number of sentences per 100 words on graph to determine the grade level of the material. Choose more passages per book if great variability is observed and conclude that the book has uneven readability. Few books will fall in gray area but when they do grade level scores are invalid.

Count proper nouns, numerals and initializations as words. Count a syllable for each symbol. For example, "1945" is 1 word and 4 syllables and "IRA" is 1 word and 3 syllables.

EXAMPLE:	SYLLABLES	SENTENCES
1st Hundred Words	124	6.6
2nd Hundred Words	141	5.5
3rd Hundred Words	158	6.8
AVERAGE	141	6.3

READABILITY 7th GRADE (see dot plotted on graph)

FIG. 4–1. *Fry graph for estimating readability—extended. (Developed by Edward Fry, Rutgers University Reading Center, New Brunswick, N.J. 08904)*

will help you estimate the "fit" of a patient's word-recognition skills to the available health instruction materials.

NOTE ON TESTING ORAL MATERIALS

There is no universally accepted way to test the degree of difficulty in oral materials. However, it is believed that some of the same characteristics that are critical for written materials will also affect the comprehensibility of spoken language. Until better measures are suggested, you might convert a spoken message (a taped segment would be useful) into written form and then apply a standard readability formula to the printed text.

Spoken language contains some additional cues that are not present in written text (tone, stress, gestures, etc.), but the spoken word also lacks other signals (punctuation, capital letters, etc.). These features may affect comprehension, but we have no conclusive data to suggest what helps or hinders or in what ways things change.

Comprehension is **not** ensured for patients with low literacy skills when the message is presented on audio tape! Many patients with low literacy skills do not possess the language or thinking skills needed to process complex and abstract ideas in **any** form. More than just word-recognition skills are required. These patients need pictures or demonstrations, or both, to make ideas concrete. It is probable that when there is a given message for a patient to learn, the patient may need to be exposed to several repetitions and multiple forms of the same message. There will be a more complete discussion of this point in Chapter 5.

REFERENCES

Bormuth J: Readability: A new approach. Reading Research Quarterly pp 79–132, 1966

Felker DB: Document Design: A Review of the Relevant Research, pp 69–93. Washington, DC, NIE/DHEW, American Institutes for Research, April, 1980

Fry E: A readability formula that saves time. In Classroom Strategies for Secondary Reading, pp 29–35. Newark, DE, International Reading Association, 1977

Fry E: Fry's Readability Graph: Clarifications, validity, and extension to level 17. Journal of Reading pp 242–252, December, 1977

McLaughlin GH: SMOG—grading—a new readability formula. Journal of Reading 12:639–646, December, 1969

Rosenshine B: New correlates of readability and listenability. In Figorel JA: Reading and Realism, pp 710–716. Newark, DE, International Reading Association, 1969

Seels B, Dale E: Readability and Reading: An Annotated Bibliography. Newark, DE, International Reading Association, 1971

CHAPTER FIVE

Tips on Teaching Patients

Teaching patients with low literacy skills about the treatment for their disease is indeed teaching as if their lives depended on it . . . and that may just be the case. The focus is on the information needed to solve the problems the patient may have in carrying out the required regimen. Emphasis is on patient participation, encouraging the patient to think through solutions or to find ways of coping with problems the regimen may present. Reward through words of support and encouragement is of critical importance for motivation and continued performance.

STEPS IN PLANNING YOUR TEACHING STRATEGY

The following are four steps you can use in planning your teaching strategy:

1. Teach the **smallest amount** possible to do the job.
2. Make your point as vivid as you can.
3. Have the patient **restate** and demonstrate the information.
4. Review repeatedly.

That's it in a nutshell—but of course there's a lot behind each of these four steps. Let's look at each of them, one at a time.

Step 1. Teach the Smallest Amount Possible to Do the Job

What is the bottom line for your teaching? What is that core of knowledge and skill without which your patient might be seriously impaired, uncomfortable, or in a life-threatening situation? You'll have to give that careful thought. Think survival.

Although an occasional patient may want to know everything that is known about his disease, most do not. What they want is to be free of pain and to be able to do the things that they have always done. Your major goal as a patient educator is to help the patient make the decisions that will keep him on the right track.

There are three objectives in teaching the smallest amount possible to do the job:

1. Your patient must **know** enough about his condition to understand the nature and the continuity of the treatment.
2. Your patient will need the relevant information to carry out the appropriate **behavior.**
3. Your patient must **want** to cooperate with the treatment.

Most patient instruction has a heavy concentration on the first objective, the knowledge goal. For example, drug information usually follows this pattern:

Purpose
Dosage
Side-effects
Specifics

We offer two suggestions at this point: reexamine the **amount of information** and **the order** in which information is given. The skill objective or the behavior you want should come first because you have to get your message across in the few minutes during which you have the patient's attention. Think in terms of the patient's point of view.

What do I take?
How much do I take?
When do I take it?
What will it do for me?
What do I do if I get a side-effect?

Once you have given the patient the information, ask the patient to "walk through" his day with you. Have him tell you in his own words what he plans to do, how often he'll do it, and whatever other specific instructions you have given him. When he is able to give you back your instruction accurately, without hesitation, and in his own words, you have confidence that comprehension has taken place.

Research on Recall   Recall is very important in developing comprehension. Joyce and his associates (1969) and Ley and Spelman (1965) indicate a loss of perhaps half of the physician's statements almost immediately after the visit. There was no relationship between recall and the patient's satisfaction with the visit. Very high and very low levels of anxiety were associated with low levels of recall.

Svarstad's study (1974) of patient–physician encounters showed that 62% of a sample of patients, when asked to explain the meaning of words taken from the transcript of their own visit the week before, could not explain the meaning of at least one word. Words missed included "hypertension," "high blood pressure," "potassium," and "sodium." Yet, during the initial interview, only 15% admitted or otherwise indicated that they did not understand one or more terms.

These studies probably confirm your own experiences in teaching patients. What efforts have been made to improve recall? Bradshaw and associates (1975) conducted three experiments on advice about developing self-control in patients' eating behavior. A total of 116 patients, male and female, were involved. Using specific instructions rather than general principles and rules, recall was boosted by over 200%. Their conclusions are that "specific instructions have a greater probability of being recalled, whether or not rules accompany them, and there is no evidence that the omission of the general rules or principles detracts from this probability." Rogers (1971) also shows that it is usually possible to adopt and use a new behavior without having knowledge of the principles. Principles knowledge enables people to judge future changes to achieve competency on a long-term basis.

Our observation of instructional sessions and review of many patient education materials show that the how-to-do-it portions of instruction often come last and tend to be brief. Rogers points out that when the required behavior changes are relatively complex, such as changes in one's diet, the amount of how-to-do-it knowledge needed for proper adoption is much greater than that for simple changes. Also, when an adequate level of how-to knowledge is not obtained prior to trying out the change, rejection or discontinuance is likely to result.

Save your teaching of principles, general rules, historical background, and the supplementary information for those patients who ask for it or who show motivation to learn "as much as I can." Many patients do not stay in an instructional mode long enough to comprehend the principles portion of an instruction.

Vocabulary Motivation for patients may be enhanced by teaching them vocabulary. You can make a big difference in compliance and continued performance by such instruction.

The vocabulary that the patient will need to learn in order to manage his problem should be included in the "smallest amount" possible to do the job. You might want to think of developing a "vocabulary kit" so that your patients will have the words to communicate about their condition or problems. Not only does the patient need to follow your directions, but you also will need his feedback for continuing clinical management.

A beginning vocabulary kit for diabetes instruction could look something like this:

Diabetes
Insulin
Symptoms
Normal
Level

For a given instructional session, use words related to the survival needs of your patient. Keeping in mind the limited storage in short-term memory (discussed in Chap. 2), teach no more than seven words at a given session.

Once you have your list of words, you may teach them by using direct verbal instruction or by making and using an audio tape (see Chap. 7). For direct verbal instruction, start by making a set of old-fashioned flash cards using a half sheet of typing paper or 3 × 5 cards and a felt-tip pen. Print each of the words on a separate sheet, as shown in Figure 5-1.

In printing the cards, use lower case letters, not capital letters, because unskilled readers need the differentiation in size and shape of letters to help them in reading.

Show the cards one at a time to the patient. For example, say "symptoms" to the patient when you show him the card

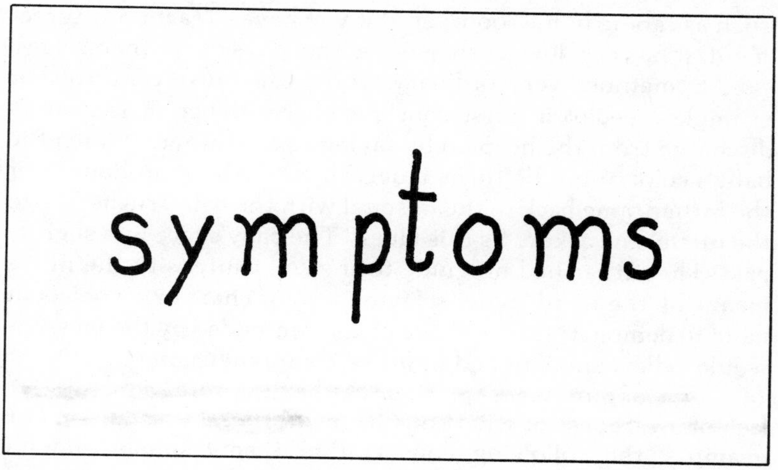

FIG. 5–1.   Sample of a flash card.

with "symptoms" written on it. Ask the patient to say the word. Then you say the word again, and ask him to say it again. Then explain the meaning of the word and how the patient may hear it used. If another term is used interchangeably with "symptoms," this is the time to teach the patient the other term or terms so that he can associate them.

When the five words with which you started your instruction are understood by the patient, go on and review additional common words that he may not comprehend in the context in which you may be using them. For example,

Cloudy insulin
Right strength
Marked by color
Alcohol wipes
Odd numbers
Even numbers
Scale
Dosage

Common nontechnical language can easily be a source of confusion, even for good readers. Wile and co-workers (1979) studied common nontechnical language to determine congruence between physicians and patients on words and phrases such as "going home soon," and "if you have a reaction." Agreement was very low even among the physicians themselves.

Sometimes very ordinary words can cause concern. For example, a pediatric nurse concluded her instruction at a baby's discharge from the hospital by saying to the father, "Watch the baby's color and if he turns blue, call me." About an hour later the father came back to the hospital with the baby, rushed up to the nurse, and asked, "Is this blue?" The baby's face was slightly pale. The father had no guide to the color intensity the nurse meant by the word "blue." Having a color chart or an object at hand to demonstrate the shade of color intended by the message would relieve anxiety and improve comprehension.

One of our biggest problems as health professionals is our lack of awareness of what constitutes technical vocabulary. For example, the following conversation seems simple enough when it starts out:

Discharge nurse: The doctor explained the baby's formula to you, didn't he?

New mother: No, ma'am.

Discharge nurse: What! I'm sure he must've told you how to fix her formula!

New mother: No, ma'am.

Discharge nurse: Well didn't the nurse explain the formula to you?

New mother: No, ma'am . . . nothing like that . . .

Discharge nurse: You mean nobody has told you how to fix the baby's milk?

New mother: Oh, yeah, that they done told me that. But not that other thing . . . fo . . . for . . . form . . .

Terms such as "formula" are not within the fluency range of many patients and they do not make fast associations of terms they may know with ones that are unfamiliar. Another problem is an inability to differentiate between terms with opposite meanings. For example, if you are teaching the motions "push" and "pull," have the patient demonstrate each motion. Do likewise with terms such as the "bottom" and the "top" of a bottle or syringe. The instruction, "If you see air bubbles, flick the syringe with your finger right at the bubbles," may need a demonstration by you of the strength and the direction of the finger motion implied in the verb "flick."

Technical terms can be learned by patients with low literacy skills, and if these terms are used in your situation, teach the terms so that the patient understands them. "Hypoglycemia" can be remembered when you stress the syllables and associate the "o" in "hypo" with the same sound in "low." You can make up your own mnemonic devices to help patients remember the few critical technical words needed.

Sometimes we may think that the mere exposure of hearing the same words used over and over again will result in understanding. Unfortunately, that is not the case. Accurate learning results from accurate teaching.

Step 2. Make Your Point as Vivid as You Can

Written material may not be vivid at all to patients. It may be incomprehensible! Therefore, you may have to tell your story in more than one way. But because written material is the most commonly used medium in patient education and contains information useful for the design of other media, you may wish to start with the printed word. We'll discuss other formats later on.

To make a message vivid:

☐ **Use simple** language and take the reader's
   present knowledge into account. Avoid jargon,
   technical vocabulary, and long explanations.

For example, consider the following instruction:

This schedule is followed until a response is exhibited.
Your dosage may then be adjusted to a dose adequate to
sustain a remission of disease activity.*

The instruction might be more clearly stated and more comprehensible in words such as, "When you start getting better, we may change this dose."

*Chrysotherapy for Rheumatoid Arthritis. Pittsburgh, St.
Margaret Memorial Hospital Patient Education
Instructions.

To improve vividness:

☐ Make your sentences **short** and **precise,** and use the active instead of the passive voice, that is, "Take your medicine before breakfast" is easier to understand than "Medicine should be taken before breakfast."

☐ Use straightforward logic and condense the message. Headings and topic sentences help the reader to organize the message. We'll discuss this point in more detail later on.

☐ **Illustrate** the important points with simple line-drawings, examples, or case studies with which the patient can identify.

☐ Summarize the important points clearly.

As we mentioned in Chapter 2, all of us have a very tight limit on the number of units of new information that we can handle when these new units are disconnected from our personal experiences. Typically not more than five to seven discrete items can be remembered unless they are combined and organized in a meaningful way. Let's illustrate how this can be done. Ley (1973) has shown that organizing material into categories and using category names can increase recall (this is well known in the reading and literacy field, but has not been emphasized in the health community). He conducted an experiment to increase patients' recall by explicitly organizing the material presented to them.

The material consisted of the following statements:

1. You have a chest infection.
2. Your larynx is slightly inflamed.
3. But I think your heart is all right.
4. We will do some heart tests to make sure.
5. We will need to take a blood sample.
6. And you will have to have your chest x-rayed.
7. Your cough will disappear in the next two days.
8. You will feel better in a week or so.
9. And you will recover completely.
10. We will give you an injection of penicillin.

11. And some tablets to take.

12. I'll give you an inhaler to use.

13. You must avoid cold drafts.

14. And you must stay indoors when the weather is foggy.

15. You must take two hours of rest each afternoon.

All of these statements were categorized into "chunks" that the patient could remember, and then the physician started out the instruction by telling the patient what the "chunks" or categories were. He said,

> I am going to tell you:
> ☐ What is wrong with you
> ☐ What tests we are going to carry out
> ☐ What I think will happen to you
> ☐ What treatment you will need
> ☐ And what you must do to help yourself

Then he took each category beginning with "what is wrong with you" and gave the information. Recall of the material was increased by nearly 50% as a result of this "chunking."

We learn from messages when we are tuned in to them, and when their information is personally important to us. If the patient thinks, "None of that is what I need," as the patient thought about those flu shots in Chapter 1, he tunes out the message. This also happens if the message begins with a historical perspective, such as

> Gout drove a Roman general to suicide, forced Henry VI to change the date of his wedding, and was responsible for Martin Luther's bad temper.*

For many patients this historical perspective would be viewed as irrelevant, and will increase the probability that they will view the following messages as also irrelevant.

Although most adults can remember five to seven items, when they are under stress they tend to remember fewer items.

*About Gout, a Form of Arthritis. Arthritis Foundation, 3400 Peachtree Road, N.E., Atlanta, GA 30326.

For this reason, try to introduce no more than three or four points before providing a chance to restate and demonstrate the new information.

If you are teaching a complex task such as filling an insulin syringe, have the patient repeat the demonstration several times to make certain that he can comprehend each of the steps and carry them out. When he can perform the task without hesitation and with accuracy, you can move ahead. Whenever you can, relate the new task to what the patient already knows and does. This facilitates comprehension and provides for reinforcement.

If you want to be sure a patient understands your message and can follow your instructions, the following are the steps that will help for the **short-term memory retention:**

□ Provide a few facts about **his particular condition.**

□ **Illustrate** the facts and **demonstrate** the activity.

□ Ask the patient to tell you what you've said **in his own words** and have him demonstrate the activity.

□ Do this repeatedly **as you go along;** don't wait until you've presented the whole message, or you'll "pour out more coffee than his cup can hold!"

When you have this worked out, you're ready for Step 3, and the **long-term memory sequence.**

Step 3. Have the Patient Restate or Demonstrate After a Time Interval

The above steps will help you to be sure that your message is in the patient's "short-term" memory for immediate recall. To transfer this information to the patient's long-term memory requires repeated practice over a period of time. Time intervals permit the integration of learning into long-term memory. Only integration into **long-term memory** will give you some hope that you can affect the patient's behavior outside of your setting.

Comprehension is confirmed when the patient can convert your language into his language. Therefore, to check on short-term memory and to provide the practice needed for long-term retention, provide opportunities for the patient to restate the ideas in his own words and to demonstrate in his own ways.

Let's take a look at this episode and think about how the mother and the staff might have relieved a painful situation if the mother had demonstrated her understanding of the recommended treatment:

> A mother brought her baby into clinic with scabies and was given soap and an ointment for treatment. She used the ointment, but the condition worsened.
>
> When she returned to the clinic, the doctor accused her of not using the ointment. After considerable discussion the mother learned that she was supposed to wash the scabs off with the soap **before** applying the ointment.

Demonstrations show the comprehension of the sequence of the steps to be taken, which in this case was critical for treatment.

Organizing the Instruction

Often you may have a number of things for the patient to keep in mind, so the questions arise, "How do I organize or present them? Does it make any difference what comes first?" Yes, the organization can make a difference. Generally it is best to group or organize instructions with the most critical action first, and the most important detail heading the list in each category.

Variety Through Patient Interaction

We realize how important variety is in teaching, and repetition can be dull. One way of getting the patients to think about the problems they may face in carrying out their regimen is to encourage the patients to share information in a group situation. How some have met and coped with difficult situations may help newer patients, and, incidentally, having patients share information in a group situation may be one of the more effective ways you can find out from some low literacy patients what may be bothering them.

Another way to get more meaningful interaction might be to plan to use at least the last 10 or 15 minutes of an instruction for a rehearsal by the patients on how they're going to explain what they've just learned to their family. If you have several patients, have them work in pairs and explain what they've just learned to one another. The instructor should monitor these interactions. Later, have them share what they have learned with the whole group.

The more patients can rehearse and see themselves in a real-life situation, the greater the chances for long-term memory retention and compliance. This kind of sharing can work well with patients with a mixed socioeconomic background and with a mix of reading skill levels.

Step 4. Provide for Repeated Reviews

Even though each section of your instructions seemed to be understood, ask your patient to summarize and demonstrate the whole procedure as a final check on your teaching and on his learning. Of course, this need not be done from memory alone. Encourage the patient to use teaching aids such as pictures or booklets in these reviews.

Suppose you are a dietitian and want to review your diet instruction with a patient or a group of patients. You have food models available for teaching purposes. Patients could demonstrate for you very quickly what they comprehend if you set up the models in a cafeteria mode and have them go down the line and select a meal based on their diet prescription. You could test their comprehension on a variety of foods by asking them to make other choices or substitutions.

Suppose you don't have food models available. In working with Arapaho and Shoshone Indians, we have used construction paper and felt-tip pens and had patients draw pictures of foods. Not only did they make some good pictures, but we were able to find out where problems in understanding still existed. Incidentally, as well as providing a useful activity, drawing is an activity that often reduces stress. This experience may not work in all cultures, but it can help in bridging language barriers.

Whenever possible, have the patient enact the instruction for you. Of course, exercises are a natural for this suggestion because the patient can physically demonstrate the motions.

Diaries and records are other forms of review, but record-keeping is beyond the knowledge and skill level of patients with low literacy skills. Calendars have little meaning for people who do not sequence information. When you give future appointment dates and times, have the patient repeat the date, the day of the week, and the time.

Instruction and review that are distributed over time are more effective than the same content compressed into a single session. If you have a patient who is hospitalized for a period of time, the various staff members who instruct the patient should space their presentations across the hospital stay, if at all possible. Time intervals permit integration of learning for the patient.

If you are working with outpatients, pick only the **most** important information for teaching during the initial visit. Let your patient know about the sequence of instructions and how you plan to space your instruction and review. This helps build continuity and can be positive motivation—the patient will know what to expect.

If you are in an institution such as a Veterans' Administration hospital where your patients may come back repeatedly, you may have an opportunity to review experiences that the patients are having. For example, consider the remarks of a patient who returned to the hospital on one of his regular visits and said, "Seems like I'm taking medicine instead of eating. That's my life now with this diet." He did not comprehend food exchanges and was eating the same menu day after day.

COMMUNITY PARTICIPATION

Providing repeated reviews for your patients can be accomplished through the use of volunteers in the community. For those in public health work, some church and civic groups may become quite interested in helping you to meet some of the literacy problems your patients face. For example, volunteers might take patients to grocery stores to help them learn how to read labels for low sodium content or other key information on labels. They can also help patients by visiting drug stores with them to help them learn how to get prescriptions filled. We have encountered patients who did not know that a prescription form was the key to obtaining their prescription drugs.

Not all of the teaching in "field" situations has to be carried out by you. True, you need to be sure of the minimum essentials learned, but reinforcement by volunteers in the community can expand and amplify the learning.

CONCLUSION

In summary, the following are the principles we have discussed:

- ☐ Don't overstuff. Limit yourself to the essentials.
- ☐ Give a little—get a little. Feedback and practice are the methods by which the learning takes place.
- ☐ Three or four items of instruction are enough at any one time for patients.
- ☐ Space the learning. Understanding takes time and practice.
- ☐ Anxiety is the enemy. Do everything you can to help your patients overcome it.
- ☐ Reward every possible step with encouraging words. Patients need all the help they can get!

Now, review for yourself the points in this chapter that are important for your kind of teaching.

What steps could you follow to create and use an instructional unit?

How could you make a message vivid?

What are some principles of learning that could be useful?

If you aren't able to close your eyes and restate these in your own words, they are probably not in your short-term memory. Go back and review the essential ideas. Practice saying them to yourself in your own words so that they are transferred to your long-term memory. Only then will they influence your personal teaching and professional work.

REFERENCES

Bradshaw P, Ley P, Kincey J: Recall of medical advice: Comprehensibility and specificity. Br J Soc Clin Psychol 14:55–62, 1975

Joyce CRB, Cople G, Mason M, et al: Quantitative study of doctor communication. Q J Med 38, No. 150:183–194, April, 1969

Ley P, Spelman MS: Communication in an outpatient setting. Br J Soc Clin Psychol 4:5, 1965, as quoted in Podell RN: Physician's Guide to Compliance in Hypertension, p 25. Merck & Co, Inc, 1975

Ley P, Bradshaw PW, Eaves D, Walker CM: A Method for increasing patients' recall of information presented by doctors. Psychological Medicine 3:217–220, 1973

Rogers M, Shoemaker FE: Communications of Innovations: A Cross-Cultural Approach, 2nd ed, pp 106–107. New York, Free Press, 1971

Svarstad B: The Doctor–Patient Encounter: An Observational Study of Communication and Outcome. Unpublished Doctoral Dissertation, University of Wisconsin, 1974, as quoted in Podell, RN: Physician's Guide to Compliance in Hypertension, p 39. Merck & Co, Inc, 1975

Wile MZ, et al: Physician–Patient Communication: Interpretations of Non-Technical Phrases. Paper presented at Association of American Medical Colleges, Washington, DC, 1979

CHAPTER SIX
Writing and Rewriting

Written instructions are used extensively in the health field. Patients are given pamphlets and booklets that describe admission procedures, disease processes, medications, and diet regimens, as well as a wide range of other topics. We expect patients to take some responsibility to learn from these materials because we often have so little time for one-to-one instructions. How well do these written instructions serve?

Written instructions from public and private sources vary widely in reading difficulty, and the degree of understanding of the instructions by the patients will also vary. A sample of 291 health instructions, many of them used nationwide, were assessed for reading level. The reading levels ranged from fourth to 16th grade, with the mean at the tenth grade level (Fig. 6-1). Fewer than 10% of the materials were at the seventh-grade reading level or lower. Thus, virtually none of these instructions will be understood by patients with low literacy skills. Even patients with average reading ability will have difficulty with over half of the materials. Clearly, there is a mismatch between the reading skills of the patients and the literacy demands of the written instructions the patients are supposed to read and understand.

This chapter presents strategies for writing health instructions that are more easily understood by a wide audience. Guidelines are given on how to plan as well as on how to write for low literacy levels. Rewriting methods are also presented. Special problems, such as the simplification of medical forms and procedures and the presentation of administrative information, are also discussed.

SIMPLIFYING TEXT

There is still considerable debate in the reading community as to exactly what characteristics make text easy to

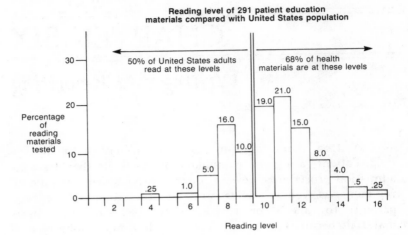

FIG. 6-1.   *Reading level of 291 health instructions. (Patient Learning Associates, Inc., Potomac, MD, Assessment 1979–1981)*

read. Readability formulas are one analytical tool used to assess reading levels of texts, but it is widely agreed that simply writing for a low "score" from the formulas will not, in itself, improve the comprehensibility of the texts.

At this point it is worth making the distinction between the mechanics of reading and the process of understanding. To read—in a mechanical sense—we must simply have the skills to decode symbols that we call words and letters. But to understand what is read (decoded) we must also share with the writer an understanding of the logic implied in the passage, and we must have sufficient experience with the subject discussed and a working knowledge of the language used. For example, many highly literate professionals in other fields would be able to decode, but not understand, a research paper on astronomy or nuclear physics. These failures to read with understanding are hardly surprising; however, similar failures are equally common among patients who do not understand health instructions (see additional data in Chap. 2).

We can learn to write our instructions so they are most easily read by the widest possible audience. An essential step to accomplish this is planning.

The Planning Steps

Before proceeding with the task of writing or rewriting, some planning can be done that will make your task easier. The planning steps are the following:

- ☐ List the patient's behavior changes or knowledge you want the instruction to help achieve.
- ☐ Decide on the relevant essential information needed by the patient to achieve the behavior or new knowledge.
- ☐ Select the method or methods to best present the information.
- ☐ Organize the topics.
- ☐ Decide on the reading level required.

Let us now examine each of these steps in turn.

Establish Behavioral Objectives and New Knowledge Required   Behavorial objectives are defined as those actions we want the patient to **do** or **know** to manage his disease or condition. New knowledge is that which is needed to achieve the behavioral objectives and to motivate the patient. Your instructional sequence should flow naturally once you can clearly state the outcome you want by indicating what the patient will **do** or **know** after instruction. Such a statement should include the observable or testable outcome and should state a criterion for acceptable performance, when appropriate. For example, a knowledge objective designed to ensure that your patient will know what causes lower back pain might read as follows:

Patient will describe the standing, sitting, and lying postures that contribute to a reduction in the frequency of lower back pain.

An objective that describes an ability to take a blood pressure reading might be written as follows:

Patient will demonstrate an ability to take own blood pressure and report systolic and dystolic pressures correctly within 5 points 4 out of 5 times.

Decide What Is Relevant Information   A broad range of printed instructions and pamphlets is available from public and private health agencies, and these instructions are often given to patients to help them understand their disease and treatment. Although many of these pamphlets are appropriate for patients with broad interests and well-developed reading skills, they are less appropriate for the millions of Americans who have low literacy skills. For them it is essential that only the most relevant information be included.

Limiting the instruction to only the most relevant information is a difficult task because so much is known that could be included. For instance, we often see instructions that start out with a history. As an example, a pamphlet on blood transfusion (NIH Publication 81-1949*) starts with, "In France and England during the 17th century transfusions were outlawed because of the disastrous effects of transfusing humans with animal blood." Later, the instruction continues with details on the physiologic process: "The plasma then carries away the waste products to your kidneys where they are excreted in your urine." How relevant would these statements be for the patient who wants to find out what he must know or do about a transfusion? The less appropriate information is likely to be counterproductive because it obscures the more important parts of the instruction. The extraneous information about animal blood creates confusion.

Our experience in examining 291 sets of patient education instructions prepared by public and private agencies shows that these instructions are likely to be inappropriate for people with low literacy skills. For these patients you need to prepare your own instructions or rewrite existing instructions.

Select Methods   Select a method of presentation that is most appropriate for your patient's learning objective. Combinations of text with visuals, demonstrations, models, or audio tapes generally reinforce learning. For example, to show a sequence of actions you expect the patient to perform, a series of line-drawings, each with a brief explanation alongside, is likely to be most suitable. Even for poor readers, the text (in combination

---

*Blood Transfusions: Benefits and Risks. Medicine for the Layman, pp 7, 9. US Department of Health and Human Services, Public Health Service, National Institutes of Health, January, 1981 (NIH, 81-149)

with other forms of display) is likely to be useful because a good friend or family member may help them.

Organize Content   Organization may be quite straightforward if a logical sequence is inherent in the instruction, such as for an exercise sequence for arthritis patients. Where there is no obvious sequence, present the most important instruction topic first or last because we tend to remember information better when it is placed first or last. If the topics seem to be of equal importance, it is often best to present the more general information first and then progress to the particular, using the general information as a base on which to build. If there is doubt as to the most effective sequence, a useful technique is to use a storyboard approach to the development of your instruction.

The storyboard approach is a topical method to plan and develop an instruction, or story. Start by making a list of topics that need to be included. Don't be concerned with the sequence at this point. Make a separate sheet for each topic, with the important information summarized for that topic along with a sketch of the visual (if used). A series of these storyboard sheets make up the entire instruction. You can experiment with many arrangements or sequences of these individual sheets. A draft storyboard sheet that might fit in the middle of an instruction on low-sodium diets is shown on Figure 6-2. When you have a sheet for each topic in draft form, arrange them in some logical order and review them with a colleague. Then pretest the storyboard sheets, while still in draft form, with a few patients.

Decide on the Reading Level   Deciding on the reading level for your instruction may present a dilemma. If the reading level you decide on is too high, many of the patients won't be able to read or understand the material; if it is too low, you may be concerned that the instruction may appear too basic for more skilled readers. Short of testing each patient's skills using the Wide Range Achievement Test (WRAT) or some other method (see Chap. 3 for methods), one approach is to assume that your patient population has reading skills similar to the national norm (in the United States) as shown in Table 6-1.

To cover this wide range of reading skills, you have two basic options: develop your instruction at the fifth-grade level, the lowest reasonable common denominator, or develop two sets of instructions, one at the fifth-grade level or lower and

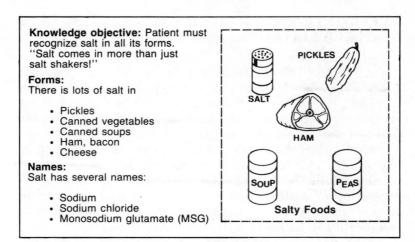

Knowledge objective: Patient must recognize salt in all its forms. "Salt comes in more than just salt shakers!"

Forms:
There is lots of salt in

- Pickles
- Canned vegetables
- Canned soups
- Ham, bacon
- Cheese

Names:
Salt has several names:

- Sodium
- Sodium chloride
- Monosodium glutamate (MSG)

FIG. 6–2.   Sample draft storyboard for part of an instruction on low-sodium diets.

one at the ninth- or tenth-grade level for readers with higher reading skills.

The second option leads to yet another dilemma: short of testing each patient, how could you know which instruction level to give to any one patient? One approach to avoid testing each patient's reading skills is to let the patient select the instruction he prefers. Matching the instruction level to the patient's reading skill level is a difficult task. Some mismatch is almost inevitable and may be remedied by subsequent instructions, perhaps with a different presentation method (see Chap. 5, Tips on Teaching Patients).

Table 6–1.
Approximate Reading Skills (USA)

Percent of Adult Population	*Approximate Reading Level*
20	@ 5th grade or below
35	@ 5th to 10th grade
45	Above 10th grade

(Roth E: APL: A ferment in education. American Education 12, No. 4:6–9, May, 1976)

WRITING FOR ADULTS
WITH LOW LITERACY SKILLS

There is an extensive literature on the art of writing. Although there is increasing public and professional awareness of the need for clear language,* unfortunately most authors do not specifically address the problem of writing for adults with low literacy skills. The following guidelines combine the most appropriate recommendations of the literature with the experiences of the authors in teaching adults with low literacy skills (Flesch, 1949, 1962; Jarmul, 1981; Miller, 1975; Pett, 1976; Shuy, 1975, 1976, 1978; Sticht, 1975).

Write in a Conversational Style

If one could choose only one from among the many techniques of writing for a low reading level and the best comprehension, it would be, "Write in active voice in a conversational style." For example:

Less Appropriate	More Appropriate
The RH system constitutes another major blood group antigen system of the red blood cells relevant to transfusions. (NIH, #81-149, p. 11)	You need to know about a blood group called "Rh" if you're going to give blood or have a blood transfusion.
Sometimes advertising for over-the-counter drugs on radio, television, or in the newspapers exaggerates the need for a drug or creates a problem for you that does not exist, or promises more results than you can expect. (We want you to know about medicines without prescriptions. HEW (FDA) 74-3010)	When it comes to drugs, don't believe everything you hear or see in the ads.

*Several states have passed plain language laws for contracts and loan agreements: New York, New Jersey, Connecticut, Maine, Hawaii, Minnesota, West Virginia.

It is easier to understand sentences written in the active voice and the message becomes more imperative. Phrases such as "The patient should . . ." are more effective when written as, "You should . . . ." After you have written your instruction, it is useful to read it aloud and to listen for naturalness and clarity. Is this the way you would explain it to a good friend? Would your patients understand these words?

The following are some additional guidelines that will help you write for lower reading levels:

☐ Use short words and short sentences—if they sound natural.

☐ Keep the concept density low.

☐ Use advance organizers.

☐ Use words consistently.

☐ First sentence is the topic sentence.

☐ Build in reviews.

☐ Build in feedback.

Let's examine each of these guidelines in turn.

Use Short Words and Short Sentences   Short words and words with fewer syllables are generally easier to read and understand. Furthermore, short words are more likely to be included in the vocabularies of people with low literacy skills. For example, write "doctor" instead of "physician" and "use" rather than "utilize." The use of more familiar words is not "talking down" to the patient. Some of the most brilliant literature, including the Bible, is written at modest reading levels.

Shorter sentences are easier to understand than long ones because for each idea or complete thought fewer words must be carried in the reader's short-term memory. Sentences with several subordinate clauses are the most difficult to read and understand. However, there is evidence (Shuy, 1978) that naturalness is more important than sentence length for ease of understanding. Consider the following example:

Original Text	**Rewritten Text**
(Approximately 15th-grade level)	(Approximately 7th-grade level)
Milk is another food of important interest. It contains a sugar, lactose, which is known chemically	Milk is another food you may have to be careful of. It contains sugar, called lactose. When some people

as a disaccharide. Certain persons with diarrheal disorders, or a history of abdominal pain, may have an inability to digest or hydrolyze this disaccharide and the ingestion of milk or milk products (or food containing milk sugar) can be followed by abdominal pain, cramping, and diarrhea, as well as increased amounts of intestinal gas. . . .

drink milk or eat food with milk products in it, they get cramps, diarrhea, or gas. . . .

(Original text from Travel Tips, Diet and the Ostomate, Insights.) Obtained from Dr. Lee Smith, Capt., Bethesda National Naval Medical Center, Bethesda, MD, 1979

The long, complex sentences are not only difficult to understand; they often "turn people off" from further reading.

Reduce Concept Density   Concept density is directly related to ease of understanding, although this factor does not show up in the reading prediction formulas. One way to reduce concept density is to limit each paragraph to a single message or action. This is difficult to do, but we usually can reduce the concept density to a main topic plus supporting facts.

An example of reducing concept density is shown below. The passage on the left is the original material in a diet manual for kidney dialysis patients. The first paragraph on the left contains 6 concepts; the second paragraph on the left contains 10 concepts. The Washington D.C. Kidney Center rewrote both paragraphs as shown on the right, and reduced the concepts to four in each paragraph.

Original

One of the vital aspects of your daily care is the adherence to a dietary regimen. Each patient's diet prescription varies, depending on the degree of

Rewritten

An important part of your daily care is your diet. Every dialysis patient is different, and your diet will be planned especially for you. Following your

kidney impairment. Accommodations to your eating habits and food preferences will be of prime importance. Successful dietary management will enhance your overall quality of life as a dialysis patient.

diet is one way to help you feel better.

Changes in a regular unlimited diet must be made because the kidneys are not able to remove waste products and excess fluid from the body now. Some of the waste products created by the foods you eat can become toxic to your body if allowed to accumulate. To create a less toxic internal environment between dialysis treatments, the intake of the sodium, potassium, protein, calories, and fluid must be carefully monitored.

The food you eat and drink makes waste products in your blood. A special diet is needed because your kidneys cannot clean these waste products from your blood. Also, your kidneys cannot remove excess fluid from your body.

Not only are the concepts reduced in number in the paragraphs on the right, but the key concepts presented are not cluttered with nonessential information.

Use Advance Organizers   Use headers or other clues as advance organizers to alert the readers as to what is coming and to focus on your intended message. If several concepts must be presented, use an advance organizer for each. An example of the effective use of advance organizers in an instruction on chronic obstructive pulmonary disease (COPD) (*Control C.O.P.D.*, nd)* is shown on the following pages.

*Control C.O.P.D., Hampton General Hospital, 3120 Victoria Blvd, Hampton, VA 23669

Advance Organizers in Chronic Obstructive Pulmonary Disease (COPD) Instruction:

Your Medications

1. The pharmacist will explain the correct way to take the medication that your physician has prescribed for you. Additionally, you must NOT take any other medications without first checking with your doctor. This especially includes:
   a. Sleeping pills (including preparations like Sominex and Sleepeze that you can buy without a prescription).
   b. Narcotics or pain relievers.
   c. Alcohol.
   d. Tranquilizers or "nerve pills."

Coughing

1. Coughing is not a sickness. Coughing is your body's way of getting rid of dust, pollution, and sputum from your lungs.
2. The Physical Therapy Department personnel will teach you more effective ways to breathe and cough up sputum.
   "Pursed lip breathing" is one way to help remove trapped air in your lungs. This is done by:
   a. Inhaling through your nose with your mouth closed.
   b. Exhaling through your mouth with your lips pursed (lips in kissing or whistling position).
   c. Making exhalation (breathing out) twice as long as inhalation.

Preventing Infection and Complications

1. Call your physician at the first sign of a cold or flu.
2. Avoid going out in extremely cold or wet weather as much as possible. If you must go out, dress warmly.

(continued)

Advance Organizers in COPD Instruction
(*continued*)
3. STOP SMOKING—This includes cigarettes, cigars and pipes.

Easier Living

1. Learn to pace yourself. Gradually increase your activities at home and rest when you become short of breath. It is important for you to be active and use your muscles so that they do not become weak. You will learn which activities you can tolerate without becoming short of breath. Your body needs oxygen for all its activities: don't waste it on useless motion.
2. When picking something up from the floor, bend from the knees rather than the waist.

(*Control C.O.P.D., pp 5–9*)

Be Consistent With Words   Use words consistently. For example, avoid interchanging "diet" with "diet prescription" and "meal plan" in the same instruction. In one instance where these words had been interchanged, some patients misunderstood and thought that the "diet prescription" was to be eaten *in addition* to their regular meals.

Put First Things First   Make the first sentence of your paragraph the topic sentence, and when possible make the first word in that sentence your topic. For example, the topic in the sentences below is "a normal life."

Less Appropriate*	More Appropriate
Once it is shown that you are a diabetic, chances are good that you can lead a normally full and productive life.	A normal life is possible for you even if you have diabetes.

*Understanding Diabetes, p 3. Pfizer Laboratories Division, Pfizer, Inc, New York, NY 10017. #SPO291X72, January, 1972

Use Feedback to Test for Learning   Ask the patient for feedback so that you may assess how well your instruction is understood. (Do **not** ask the patient, "Do you understand?") Asking for and receiving substantive feedback will also add reinforcement to the instruction you have provided. Feedback can be obtained in several ways. You can ask questions or ask the patient to solve a problem.

If the patient can translate your instruction into his own words, or if he can demonstrate the behavior desired, you have a good indication that the patient understands. A good method of doing this is to ask the patient to explain the instruction to another patient while the instructor monitors the explanation for accuracy.

Summarize and Review   Health instructions, like most other kinds of instructions, require summary and review if they are to be learned. One approach to doing this is to present the same information in a different form. In the example presented below, we see a question-and-answer form used to summarize and review a preceding text. The example, from *Health Care for Seafarers: A Guide to Care and Services,** was published by the Public Health Service. This section deals with the complex conditions for eligibility of care. Note that the questions are posed from the patient's point of view.

Q. If I am injured aboard ship on my first day of duty, am I eligible for emergency PHS care?

A. Yes. When you are employed on a ship you are eligible for emergency care regardless of length of service.

Q. If I have worked for 60 days, but not on the same vessel, am I still eligible?

A. Yes, you are.

Q. What if I have had a break in work during the past year?

A. If you have 60 days of service and the break is less than 180 days, you are still eligible for PHS care.

The technique is to take each instance or circumstance and treat it as a single unit of information, using a conversational style.

*HHS, Pub. No (HSA) 80-2016 (Rev. June 1, 1980)

REWRITING; HOW TO SIMPLIFY THE TEXT

Very often you may already have material with the information you need for an instruction, but the material may be too difficult for your patients to understand. Start from what you have to prepare your simplified version.

First decide on the patient behavior desired. Circle the information in your original material that is essential to achieve the desired behavior in the patient. Organize the topics in the sequence the patient needs to use the information. Use an active voice and a conversational style to rewrite the essential information. Use advance organizers, and build in feedback. Repeat or summarize. Pretest with a sample of your patients. Ask them to tell you in their own words or to show you by demonstration what they think the instruction means.

SPECIAL PROBLEMS

Two kinds of text are most difficult to write at low reading levels. These are (1) instructions dealing with administrative procedures where a legal issue is involved and (2) forms, such as consent forms for treatment.

Administrative procedures are almost always written in a passive voice, and sentences often carry one or more conditional clauses. Breaking the long sentences down to several shorter ones may help, but this is often not satisfactory for those accustomed to the style of legal language. The simplification guidelines mentioned earlier can be applied, but it is often helpful to ask yourself the question, "What is the intent of this instruction?" An example of how the authors reduced the reading level of one section of the Public Health Service's *Health Care for Seafarers** booklet is given below:

Original Text	Rewritten Text
Approximately 16th-Grade Level	Approximately 9th-Grade Level
It should be understood that any authorization	Even when the PHS does give a telephone OK for

*HHS, Pub. No. (HSA) 80-2016 (Rev. June 1, 1980)

given will be conditioned upon the establishment of the seaman's eligibility through proper documentation of the sea service/injury while employed aboard a documented vessel. IF THIS ELIGIBILITY IS NOT ESTABLISHED THE PHS WILL NOT ASSUME RESPONSIBILITY FOR THE COST OF CARE. such care, you still must prove you are eligible. **This must be done before the PHS will pay your bill.**

Forms, such as the patient's consent form, are notoriously difficult to read and understand. Readability formulas do not apply very accurately because of the brevity of the text on the form. Impersonal language is used on most forms. Incomplete sentences are common. Some forms use cryptic abbreviations. To simplify forms, do the following:

□ Use an active voice.

□ Write complete sentences and avoid abbreviations.

□ Use personal pronouns rather than the impersonal.

□ Don't use nouns made from verbs such as **"Disallowance** will result from **failure** to . . ."

SUMMARY

A large percentage of the public cannot read and understand written health instructions. Few of the health instructions provided by the public and private health agencies are written below the seventh-grade reading level, which is the reading level of about one third of the adult population. If your instructions are to be understood by these patients, you probably must prepare your own.

Planning steps that will make your job of writing easier are

□ First decide on the desired patient behavior or new knowledge.

□ Decide on the most relevant information needed.

☐ Select the most appropriate presentation methods.

☐ Decide on the reading level required.

☐ Organize topics in the way the patient will use them.

To write for low literacy levels, you should

☐ Use an active voice and a conversational style.

☐ Use shorter words and sentences.

☐ Keep the concept density low.

☐ Use words consistently.

☐ Use advance organizers.

☐ Put first things first.

☐ Summarize and review.

☐ Build in feedback from the patient.

Administrative instructions and consent forms are the most difficult material to write at low reading levels. With forms, use the active voice; use personal pronouns; avoid abbreviations and nouns made from verbs.

If you learn only one message from this chapter, that message must be, "When writing for low reading levels, use a conversational style and the active voice."

REFERENCES

Blood Transfusions: Benefits and Risks. Medicine for the Layman, p 11. US Department of Health and Human Services, Public Health Service, National Institutes of Health, January, 1981 (NIH, #81-149)

Flesch RF: The Art of Readable Writing. New York, Harper & Row, 1949

Flesch RF: The Art of Readable Writing. New York, Collier Books, 1962

Jarmul D: Plain Talk: Clear Communication for International Development. Arlington, VA, Volunteers in Technical Assistance (VITA), 1981

Kern RP, Sticht T, Welty D, Hauke RN: Guidebook for the Development of Army Training Literature, Chapter 2, pp 5-11, (Topic oriented versus performance-oriented training literature); Chapter 3, pp 11-24 (Preparing to write performance-oriented training literature); Chapter 4, pp 25-30 (Your primary user's reading level

and what it means); Chapter 5, pp 31–136 (Writing and re-
vising—A before and after guide). Alexandria, VA, Human
Resources Research Organization (HumRRO), Army Project No.
2Q063101A755, November, 1976

Miller E: Designing Printed Instructional Materials: Content and
Format. Alexandria, VA, Human Resources Research Organization
(HumRRO), October, 1975

Pett D (ed): Writing, pp 80–82. In Audio-Visual Communications
Handbook. From original by Peace Corps/Indiana University,
Contract #25-1707. Oklahoma City, World Neighbors, 1976

Roth E: APL: A ferment in education. American Education 12, No.
4:6–9, May, 1976

Shuy R: The Patient's Right to Clear Communications in Health and
Mental Health Delivery Systems. Address presented at the
Conference on Health and Mental Health Systems, Philadelphia,
November 22, 1975. Arlington, VA, Center for Applied Linguistics,
Georgetown University

Shuy R: The Consumer and Insurance Policy Language. Address
presented at the Conference on Consumers and Life Insurance,
Washington, DC, May 15, 1978. Arlington, VA, Center for
Applied Linguistics, Georgetown University, 1978

Shuy R; Medical interview: Problems in communication. Primary Care
3, No. 3:365–386, September, 1976

Sticht TG (ed): Methods for reducing literacy demands of jobs. In
Reading for Working: A Functional Literacy Anthology, pp
96–110. Alexandria, VA, Human Resources Research Organization
(HumRRO), 1975

We Want You to Know About Medicines Without Prescriptions. HEW
(FDA) 74-3010

CHAPTER SEVEN
Learning From Audio Tapes

Listening is one of the primary means of learning. As much as 70% of the average adult's working day is spent in verbal communication, with 45% of that time spent in listening (Brown et al., 1977). In recognition of this, audio tapes, either alone or in combination with workbooks or filmstrips, are being increasingly used to present health instructions to patients. Taped instructions are especially important for the patients with low literacy skills and the visually impaired.

Tapes offer many advantages. They can improve comprehension and reduce learning time. They can also free the health-care providers from having to give repetitive, routine instructions. Additionally, the tapes don't "forget"; they present a standardized and complete information package with the same level of enthusiasm each time they are used.

But audio tapes carry a literacy demand also. The oral language decoding process is similar to print decoding in reading (Sticht, 1974; Tuman, 1980). Thus, for patients who have limited language skills, or for whom English is a second language, English language audio tapes may present the same obstacles as written instructions.

An assessment of the literacy demands of audio instruction tapes used in a large hospital (Doak and Doak, 1980) revealed that the tapes were beyond the language skills of over half the patients. The scripts for these tapes would have to be rewritten if more patients were to understand them. The best solution for you as a health-care provider may be to produce your own taped instructions.

One advantage of "homemade" taped instructions is that your tape can reflect the standards that apply at your institution, something a commercially made tape cannot do. Furthermore, when patients hear your voice at the clinic and later on tape, there is recognition and hence more attentive listening. Another advantage is that local language dialects, accents, and local references can be used, which enhance the relevance of your instruction. Finally, the cost of these tapes should be lower than those produced commercially.

This chapter leads the reader through the steps necessary to produce effective audio instruction tapes. Making your own tapes is both easy and satisfying, and your instruction will be far more likely to meet the needs of your patients.

A COMPARISON OF READING AND LISTENING

Similarities between reading and listening are more significant than their differences. Except for children under the age of about 12 years, there is a good correlation between the effectiveness of learning by listening and learning by reading. Good listeners tend to be good readers and vice versa. The most critical similarity is that reading and listening use the same language decoding process. Both produce a message or concept in the mind of the listener and reader.

Additional similarities are that both provide cues via their structure, grammar, sequence, and tempo, and, for comprehension, both demand attention and the exercise of memory on the part of the listener or reader. Both rely on an existing knowledge base with which to associate new information if long-term learning is to take place.

Differences between listening and reading are principally in the transient nature of speech and the tone and rhythm available in speech. Another difference is that, in listening, the rate of flow of information is usually not controllable by the listener. Visuals and graphics are not directly included on tapes or in speech the way they may be included along with the text, but sound effects may be included.

An additional difference is that language used in speech is quite different from that used in written text. Speech is more informal, more colloquial, more "natural." It offers additional variability and may carry an accent that can enhance or detract from comprehension. These characteristics can offer great advantage in learning.

Some people learn better by listening, others by reading. Thus, despite the good correlation between listening and reading as methods of learning in general, individuals often have a strong preference. This may create a dilemma for the educator: "Which method of instruction should be used?" One approach is to make both tapes and text available (with or without visuals) and then invite the patients to make their own choices. For additional information on this subject, we suggest *Language by Ear and by Eye* (Kavanagh and Mattingly, 1972), and *Auding and Reading* (Sticht, 1974).

PLANNING THE USE OF AUDIO TAPES

Audio tapes are now in vogue, especially with people under 30 years of age. Headphones are almost as common as hats on joggers, cyclists, and people just walking down the street. We have had to remind one of our adult basic reading students to remove his headphones while he was in class.

The following situations (and there are many more) are especially suitable for audio tapes used either alone or together with some other form of instruction:

- ☐ When the patient prefers to learn by listening
- ☐ For visually impaired patients
- ☐ When combined with another instruction mode, such as a companion booklet that shows pictures or a visual sequence of what is to be learned
- ☐ When there is a language difference (when English is a second language, either for the doctor or the patient, and the tape can be made in the patient's language)
- ☐ For low literacy patients who need variety to overcome an attention span problem
- ☐ To present introductory, routine, repetitive, or standardized instructions
- ☐ When sound effects can enhance the message

WHERE TO USE TAPES

Tapes are often used at the bedside of hospitalized patients. Have you considered using tapes in the waiting room for outpatients? Even in a busy waiting room patients can listen to tapes in privacy by using headphones. Such taped instruction will enhance the image of the institution as a progressive and a caring place. Even more importantly, the information supplied on the tape can initiate meaningful dialogue between patients and the health-care providers. There is newly acquired information from the tape to talk about and to share together.

PRODUCING THE MESSAGE

One of the more difficult elements in designing instructional messages is to define clearly their purpose and scope.
Try asking yourself the following questions:

- [ ] **What outcome do I want from the patient?**
- [ ] **What behavior change?**
- [ ] **What do I want the patient to do differently?**
- [ ] Finally, if I could get **only one** point across to the patient at this time, **what would it be?**

It helps to place fairly restrictive boundaries on both the scope and the expected outcomes of your instruction.

For most of us, the most effective taped instructions are less than 10 minutes' duration. Adults with low literacy skills and those with learning disabilities tend to have very short attention spans and can benefit from even shorter segments. A taped instruction nearer 5 minutes' duration is even more optimal.

Longer tapes also can be effective if they contain breaks approximately every 5 minutes so that the patient has an opportunity to recap, summarize, or respond to questions. This is also a good time for the patient to interact with questions on an accompanying worksheet. These breaks will help any listener, but they are crucial for those with poor literacy skills.

Let's assume that you have decided to provide a taped instruction on hypertension. You have selected the following purposes:

1. To explain what hypertension is
2. To convince newly diagnosed hypertensive patients that they should take their medication every day
3. To explain the role of diet in reducing hypertension

4. To explain the need for the patient to return to the clinic regularly for blood pressure measurement.

If taken all together, a continuous and detailed instruction of this scope could overload patients with low literacy skills, and little or nothing would be learned. Do you remember the limitations of short-term memory in holding new units of information that we discussed in Chapters 2 and 5?

To prevent this overload, you have planned a less detailed introductory tape. You might organize purposes 1 and 2, listed above, as shown in Table 7-1.

Once the points to be covered are decided upon, the sequence of the instruction needs to be addressed. For some instructions, this sequence is quite straightforward. For example, the sequence of interventions in cardiopulmonary resuscitation (CPR) is airway, breathing, and compression (ABC). When the sequence is less obvious, the best guideline may be to proceed from the general to the specific, determining the prerequisites needed to proceed with the next piece of information. Let's take a patient who needs more exercise. Your instruction might start with the general statement, "Get more exercise"; following this, you would proceed with the types and duration of various forms of exercise.

Questions at the end, or during the instruction, provide learning reinforcement because the tape (after a time pause) can provide the correct answers. For instance, the patient may be asked to check a multiple-choice answer in a workbook or to supply an appropriate number as in the blood pressure segment. The best questions are those that require some overt act or information converted into the patient's own words, such as, "say in your own words. . . ."

Furthermore, the questions serve to break the instruction into bite-sized chunks. These chunks are easier to associate with information already known by the patient. This is part of the chunking process for short-memory we discussed in Chapter 2.

Once the topics and questions have been decided, you have a clear blueprint to follow. At this point you can record your instruction extemporaneously. This sounds more vital and natural, and may be more easily understood than a message read from a script. Even the small imperfections and hesitations can

Table 7-1.

Sample Content for an Instruction Segment on Hypertension

Subject	Purpose	Points to Cover	Questions
Hypertension	Understand hypertension and follow medication regimen	• What is hypertension • What is patient's blood pressure • Dangers of hypertension • Taking medicine can control hypertension • Take medicine every day even when you feel OK	• What is high blood pressure? • What is your blood pressure? • Can you name one danger of high blood pressure? • How can you lower your blood pressure? • Must you take medicine every day if you feel all right?

(Adapted from Working Group to Define Critical
Patient Behaviors in High Blood Pressure Control:
Patient Behavior for Blood Pressure Control:
Guidelines for Professionals. JAMA 241, No.
23:2534–2537, 1979)

add naturalness and can enhance, rather than detract, from comprehension.

On the other hand, you may feel more comfortable if you have a script. Should you decide to write a script first, write it in the language you would use in talking with a patient. This will lead to a more conversational tone, and it is also likely to reduce the literacy demand of the instruction.

In writing the script, use short, common-usage words when they will serve (i.e., pill rather then medication). Use personal pronouns: "You should. . . ." rather than "The patient should." Vary the lengths of sentences just as you do in normal conversation. It helps to use a predictable, repetitive format. (You may note that this paragraph follows a predictable repetitive format: each instruction is followed by an example.)

Don't change a word or term just for variety. If you begin your instruction using the term "high blood pressure;" do not change to "hypertension" unless you first add an explanation for the new word. The use of tapes to teach special vocabulary needed by patients is covered later in this chapter.

Draw attention to key points in your taped instruction just as you would if you were in conversation with the patient, which in reality you are. You can do this by changing your tone of voice to a more urgent tone, by repetition, and by giving emphasis in the summary and the questions.

You may be tempted to speak more slowly when making a recording to be used with patients whom you believe have low literacy skills. However, the research shows that learning is more effective when instructions are presented at a normal rate of speech typically between 100 and 150 words per minute (Sticht, 1975).

If both sides of the tape are used in the instruction, your script should include a special message near the end of the first side of the tape that tells the listener to turn the tape over after first stopping the tape and pushing the eject button.

Now let's go to a **sample** script for the instruction segment shown in Table 7-1. The script in monologue style might read like this:

High blood pressure is often called hypertension. That means the pressure pushing on the walls of the blood vessels is too high for safety.

Your blood pressure was tested by the doctor or nurse. The larger number is the pressure when the heart is pumping. The smaller one is when the heart is resting. You need to know both numbers.

High blood pressure is dangerous. It can cause a stroke, a heart attack, or kidney failure. But you can control high blood pressure by taking your pills every day.

High blood pressure gives no warning. That's why

you've got to take your pills every day even if you feel OK.

The better you understand this, the better your chances for a healthy life. I will now ask you some questions on high blood pressure. After each question, say out loud, or to yourself, what you think is the best answer.

Question: First, what is high blood pressure? (*Pause*)
Answer: If you said something like, "It's when the blood is pushing too hard for safety," you have the right idea.

Let's try another:

Question: What is *your* blood pressure? (*Pause*)
Answer: If you could repeat the numbers the doctor or nurse told you, you are right again. If you are not sure, ask the doctor or nurse to tell you.

Ready for another?

Question: What is one danger from high blood pressure? (*Pause*)
Answer: If you said stroke, heart attack, or kidney failure, you were right.

Here's another:

Question: What do you have to do to control your high blood pressure? (*Pause*)
Answer: You are on the right track if you said "take your pills as the doctor told you."

Here's the last one:

Question: Do you have to take your pills every day even if you feel good? (*Pause*)
Answer: You're right if you said, "Yes."

By now you know

☐ That high blood pressure means there's an unsafe pressure in your blood vessels, which sometimes is called hypertension
☐ What your blood pressure is

- ☐ It can cause stroke, heart attack, or kidney failure if not controlled
- ☐ You can control high blood pressure by taking your pills
- ☐ You must take your pills every day

> If you're not sure of the numbers of your blood pressure or you have any questions, now is the time to ask your doctor or nurse to help you.

The process just described is quite simple. A key reason for its simplicity is that the message content is restricted and is presented in bite-sized segments that can be easily understood. Questions are asked of the patient after each segment to provide reinforcement and also to separate the points being covered.

The language is fairly conversational, and the words do not demand specialized vocabulary. If these factors are overlooked, patient comprehension will suffer. As an example, consider a small portion from the middle of a tape for instructing patients about gout.*

Taped Instruction	Impact on Patients With Low Literacy Skills
Everyone has uric acid in his body. But some people—people with gout—have too much uric acid. Either their bodies make too much or they don't get rid of it fast enough. Ordinarily, uric acid is dissolved in the bloodstream, but when people with gout make too much or get rid of too little, uric acid accumulates.	Clear, nonthreatening message; easily understood. Impersonal Long sentence; easier if repeated phrase, "make too much," "too little" is dropped Easier if "accumulates" is replaced by "builds up"
The blood becomes saturated beyond its	Problem: the words "in solution, precipitates,

*Gout. Tape used at Norfolk Public Health Service Hospital, Norfolk, VA, 1979.

capacity to hold acid in solution. When this happens, the uric acid precipitates out like crystals, very much the way water in saturated air in winter condenses out in crystalline snowflakes. The needle-shaped uric acid crystals have favorite places where they collect . . . ."	saturated, and condenses" assume a knowledge of physics or chemistry. Analogy (snowflakes) detracts from the subject. Clutter: patient cannot make use of "needle-shaped" fact, and it obscures more important information.

Let's examine an alternative script that covers the same subject matter, but at a reduced literacy demand. No attempt is made in this example to assess the need for this information for change in patient behavior. The intended purpose is simply to reduce the literacy demand of the script.

> . . . Everyone has uric acid in his body. It's in the blood.
> But if you have gout, you have too much uric acid.
> Either your body makes too much, or you don't get rid of
> it fast enough.
>   You have gout. That means that your blood has to get
> rid of extra uric acid. It does this by dropping it off at
> joints in your body where it piles up. . . .

The rewritten script contains essentially the same information as the original, but it is shorter. Predicted reading levels of the two scripts using the Fry test (as we discussed in Chap. 4) shows the original reading level to be between the 10th- and the 11th-grade levels, and the rewritten script to be between the third- and fourth-grade levels.

Currently there are no well-established, agreed-upon, standardized tests to predict the literacy demands of audio tapes. Because the same language skills are used for both auding and reading, a readability assessment of the script can be used to provide some measure of comparative languaging difficulty. (see Note on Testing Oral Materials, Chap. 4).

DIALOGUES

The scripts presented so far have been monologues, but dialogues can be even more interesting. The excitement of speaker interactions and the likelihood of questions and answers not only stimulate motivation to listen, but also help to reinforce learning by the listener.

The following script was transcribed from a tape made by two dietitians to describe the important role of fiber in our diets.* The dialogue is entirely extemporaneous. The running time of the tape is about 4½ minutes, almost an ideal length.

One dietitian begins the dialogue by taking the role of the patient (Pt), the other dietitian takes the role of a registered dietitian (RD).

Pt: Tell me, what is fiber?

RD: Fiber is part of the food that you do not digest.

Pt: The part of the food that I do not digest! Why should I have **this** in my diet?

RD: Fiber is good because it cleans the intestines. It works like an intestinal broom.

Pt: Intestinal broom! Ummmm . . . that's news to me. Where did you get that idea?

RD: Where I grew up, the German people called the pumpernickel bread the intestinal broom because it works like a broom. It swells up with water and pushes against the muscles and makes the muscles clean the intestines.

Pt: You're saying that . . . ahhh . . . it makes the muscles strong and healthy? That makes me think. I had a friend whose arm was broken and in a sling . . . and when it wasn't used, it made the muscles weak. Will the fiber . . . uh, that provides the bulk make the intestinal muscles strong?

RD: Yes, fiber will do this. It should be included in the diet, and you can add fiber in the foods you eat every day—like fruits and vegetables and whole-grain breads and cereals.

Pt: The fruit I eat every day, the whole-grain cereals, uhh . . . would you help me out? Uhh . . . when I

*Workshop, 1982, Maryland Dietetic Association. Conducted by Patient Learning Associates, Inc.

go to the grocery store . . . uhhh, . . . let's see now . . . what would I be picking up?

RD: Well, you can get whole-wheat bread, and you can get bran cereals. To help you along a little bit, I can give you some examples. In the morning when you get up; you can have some bran cereals and fresh fruit. For lunch, it would be wise to include a salad. And for dinner you can try things like whole-wheat bread and brown rice rather than the plain white rice.

Pt: Let's see now . . . if I heard you right . . . how would this be? If tomorrow morning I have Bran Buds and fresh peaches, am I getting fiber?

RD: Yes, you are getting fiber from the bran and the peaches.

Pt: And if I have my peanut butter sandwich on whole-wheat bread instead of white bread, am I getting fiber?

RD: Yes, exactly.

Pt: And if I include a green salad, I'm getting fiber?

RD: Yes. And you can include cucumbers, lettuce, and spinach—all of that helps.

Pt: Well . . . I think I'll try this. . . .

RD: Now, I've told you that fiber is good to eat, but you don't want to eat too much fiber, because this could cause problems such as. . . .

Pt: You're telling me to eat fiber, and now you're telling me not to eat too much! What happens if I eat too much?

RD: If you eat too much, it will cause irritation.

Pt: Irritation??

RD: Yes.

Pt: I remember. . . . Irritation. A friend of mine was telling me . . . uhh, they use a big word, you remember that big word? Diverticulosis. They meant it was like a balloon blowing out.

RD: (*Pulls balloon from beneath the table and pricks it so it bursts with a loud bang*) (*BANG.*) Fiber in a moderate amount is just right. Not enough is bad; too much is bad also. So check with your dietitian or other authority to get just the right amount.

ORGANIZING THE TIMING OF YOUR TAPE

Planning on the organization of your tape before recording can pay dividends in improved timing of your instruction and in giving you flexibility for improvements or changes later on. One way to organize your tape time is by sketching a time line. Figure 7-1 shows a time line for a 5-minute time segment.

COMBINING TAPES WITH WORKSHEETS

Learning can be more effective when multiple stimuli are used. Audio tapes can be combined with workbooks or worksheets to improve learning through feedback. The advantages of tape–workbook learning accrue not only to the patient, but also to the health-care provider who can receive a record of the acquired learning.

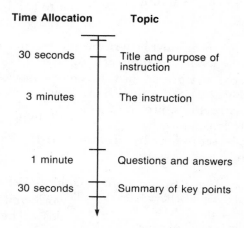

Time Allocation   **Topic**

30 seconds   Title and purpose of instruction

3 minutes   The instruction

1 minute   Questions and answers

30 seconds   Summary of key points

FIG. 7-1.   *Time line for a 5-minute segment of taped instruction.*

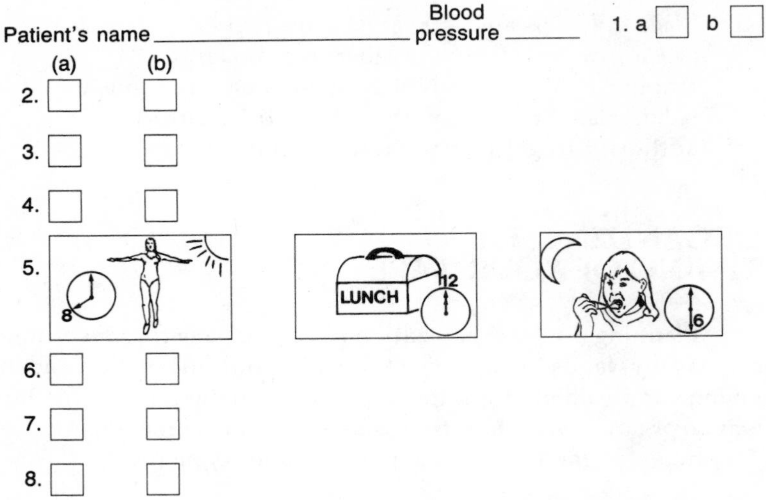

FIG. 7-2.   *Worksheet for hypertension script.*

Preparation of the tapes should follow the guidelines presented earlier in this chapter, but because of the interactions with the worksheets, a script should be prepared in advance. The script must include explicit instructions to the listener to coordinate the tape with the worksheet. The tape must include instructions such as:

> Open your workbook, titled, "Hypertension, What It Means to You," and turn to page 2. (Pause 5 seconds or so). . . .

The worksheet must be written at a reading level suitable for the patient population for which it is to be used. Worksheets and workbooks may present pictures and other visuals together with text (Fig. 7-2). Since the listener cannot ask the tape for clarifying instructions, provide a simple example of where the listener is to look, and what he is to do, at the very start. The following tape script for a hypertension instruction* illustrates these points:

> *Hypertension. Based on Working Group to Define Critical Patient Behaviors in High Blood Pressure Control: Patient Behavior for Blood Pressure Control: Guidelines for Professionals. JAMA 241, No. 23:2534–2537, 1979.

Patient Decisions: Make Decision to Control Blood
Pressure and Take Medication as Described

Script

This tape is made to help you learn about high blood
pressure and what it will mean to you. Please listen to
some information; then use the workpage when the tape
tells you to.

When we measure blood pressure we want to see how
hard the blood has to push to get to all the places it has
to go. When it pushes too hard, you could have a heart
attack, a stroke, or kidney problems unless you take
medicine to keep the pressure where it should be. If your
diastolic blood pressure is more than 105 you will need to
take medicine to stay well.

Now look at your workpage. Right after your name
are two numbers that tell you how high your blood
pressure is. Is the second number more than 105?

If it is, you are one of the people who will need to
take medicine to stay well.

This problem of high blood pressure could fool you
because it doesn't hurt, and you could even forget you
have it. But don't let it fool you . . . it's there all right,
and it probably won't go away. As long as you live, you
will need to take the medicine your doctor gives you.

But you're lucky too, because the medicine can control
your high blood pressure, although it can't cure it. That's
why you must take it every day. If you don't the
possibility of a heart attack or a stroke or kidney failure
is much more likely and taking your medicine is a lot
easier than having one of those problems.

Now look at your workpage.

Up at the top on the right-hand side, put a circle
around the second number that tells you what your
blood pressure is. OK. Now, if that number is bigger
than 105, put a check in the first box, marked (a). If it is
smaller than 105, put a check in the second box, marked
(b).

Now lets move on down the page to the left side
where you see the first two boxes and the No. 2 to the
left of the boxes. If you think that people who have high
blood pressure always feel sick, check the first box,
marked (a). If you think they may not feel sick at all,
check the second box, marked (b).

Now to the next box, No. 3. If you think you could
have a heart attack, stroke, or kidney failure if you stop

taking your medicine, check the first box. If you think you can let the medicine go if you feel all right, check the second box.

Now let's go on to the next box, No. 4 on your workpage. If you think the medicine can cure you, check the first box. If you think the medicine can't cure you, but it will make it less likely that you will develop something really serious, check the second box.

If you checked the first box for questions 1 and 3 (pause), and the second box for items 2 and 4 (pause), you were right; go on listening to the tape.

If you checked the wrong box for any of the questions, press the (yellow) button to rewind the tape and listen again.

Your doctor has figured out what medicine you will need to stay well. You will learn exactly what to do, and as long as you keep doing it every day, the chances are that you will not be bothered by your high blood pressure.

Sometimes somebody wanting to be helpful will suggest that you try something else that they are sure will be better than the medicine your doctor wants you to take. But your doctor is always looking for new treatments and would certainly know if there was a better one that is not dangerous to you. If you wonder about this, just ask your doctor first.

The person who gave you this tape will explain what medicine you are to take, and how often you are to take your medicine. If there are any problems you can see, tell this person about them so an answer to the problem can be found. There could be a problem about money for your pills, or you could be one of the few people who really have a hard time taking medicine, or there may be some other reason that you know about that might interfere with your taking the medicine every single day.

Now find the person who gave you this tape. And then come back for the rest of our talk. *(Staff member gives patient either the medication or a sample of the medication and tells the patient when and how to take the medication.)*

Now that you know which pills to take, and when, use your workpage to be sure you remember the rest of the things this tape told you about. Back now to your workpage and No. 5. Put a pill on each square which shows a part of the day during which that pill is to be taken.

Remember, your pills are your ticket to good health. Don't forget to take them every day . . . no matter what . . . and that you get a new supply **before** the bottle is empty. If your money gets low, skip something else if you have to, but don't skip your pills.

Now look at No. 6. If you think it might be a good idea to try other medicines your friends might suggest, check the first box. If you would ask your doctor first, check the second box.

OK. Let's move on now to question No. 7. If you feel you are in charge of remembering to take your medicine, and seeing that there is always a supply on hand, check the first box. If you expect there will probably be quite a few times that you may forget or be too busy with other things to bother about this, check the second box.

And now for the last question on this tape, No. 8. If you aren't too sure about always taking your medicine because there isn't always money for things like that, check the first box. If you know you can make a plan to see that you have what you need, and you know you need that medicine, check the second box.

If you checked the second box for questions 6 and 8 (pause), and the first box for question 7 (pause), you have finished with this tape.

If you did not check these boxes, there are still some problems you will need help on. It is very important to get these problems worked out before you leave here so go find the person who gave you this tape and show her your workpage so she will know how she can help. There's more to be learned, but that will be on the next tape. Give this tape back to the person who gave it to you, but be sure to show that person your workpage, too, if you need more help. Thank you.

AUDIO AND VIDEO

A few words are in order on the audio portion of video instructions. The use of these instructions has become much more widespread in hospitals and clinics, as well as in many public institutions. Many of these video instructions are fast paced to gain attention and retain interest, and they are not well designed for people with low literacy skills.

Audio is a natural, expected, and vital part of video instructions. Audio directs attention, explains the action, and. above all, carries the story. Audio can also set the mood, add human interest, and capture attention.

Planning the audio portion of the instruction is more complex than for instructions using audio alone because the audio and video must be synchronized. The planning steps are similar for both audio and video and should be done together. For both, clear definitions of the scope and goals are essential. Once the planning has been completed, a series of storyboards covering both audio and video should be developed.

Each storyboard is a one-page depiction of the purpose and topic of that scene. After storyboards for the entire instruction have been drafted, any of the storyboards may be modified, placed differently in sequence, or dropped altogether. This should be done while the storyboards are still in rough sketch form.

A script should be developed directly from the final version of the storyboard sequence. A script is usually necessary to ensure that the audio content is consistent with and reinforces the action shown on the video.

A detailed time-line diagram may be helpful to coordinate the audio and the video. It may be helpful to make a time line for many of the individual storyboards as well as for the entire instruction. For example, for a demonstration-type instruction, the time line could show pauses in the audio to allow time for the patient to concentrate on the action shown on the video.

Feedback from the patients can enhance their learning and also alert the instructor when a topic is not being understood. You can build in feedback by including questions in your script. Another approach—and this is especially appropriate for instructions of over ten minutes' duration—is to "stop the show" after a key point has been covered and then recap and ask questions before resuming.

Pretesting with at least a few patients can uncover comprehension problems with an instruction. Often, it is not necessary to remake the video portion of the instruction to correct such problems. A revision to the audio—perhaps the use of different words or an example—may clear up the problem. It is worth remembering that the audio carries the story, and you can make your story understandable by those with low literacy skills by careful planning, suitable words, and appropriate timing.

TEACHING PLANS

As in other modes of instruction, audio tapes require a little planning for their most effective use. Tapes may be the sole mode of instruction, or they may be combined with other visual, tactile, or speech forms. The decision of which combinations to use depends on the objectives of the instruction and the language capability of the patient.

For example, plan to use a two-step teaching process for patients with low literacy skills when presenting the basics or introductory information. Introductory information on diseases such as arthritis, diabetes, hypertension, or others may first be presented to the patient by audio tape, followed by person-to-person or group instruction. During the face-to-face instruction, the key points made earlier on the tape can be emphasized and the patient's questions can be answered.

A measure of the learning that has taken place, at least at the recall level, can be obtained by repeating the questions the patient heard earlier on the tape. Reinforcement and drill are essential for patients who have low literacy skills.

An audio tape heard with the privacy of headphones is one of the most nonthreatening forms of instruction. Learning is enhanced because there is no embarrassment of being wrong in front of others. Repetitions as often as the listener wishes can be obtained without asking for them.

Additional teaching plans and strategies that use audio tapes are covered in Chapter 5, Tips on Teaching Patients.

TEACHING A VOCABULARY

Audio tapes are ideal for teaching the sound and meanings of words patients need to use in discussing their problems. The drill work needed for vocabulary can be handled much more effectively with audio tapes than on a person-to-person basis. Many patients do not have a clear understanding of key medical words or of many nonmedical words that are essential to the comprehension of their health problems.

Because no standards for vocabulary have been established for any disease category,* you will have to establish your own

*The Diabetes Dictionary, available from the National Diabetes Information Clearinghouse, December, 1983,

minimum vocabulary list based on your experience and observations of what words patients must know.

If you limit your vocabulary list to just a few words, you need not make a special tape for the definitions. You can fit these vocabulary instructions right into the points you are covering.

Most of all, listen for words frequently used in your setting, and explain those words. For example if acronyms or initializations, such as IVs or ECGs, are used a great deal, explain their meaning to patients. It may be surprising to you how many of these "shorthand" expressions creep into our instructions without notice. Ask the patient to "tell me in your own words what this means" if you are tempted to find out "do you understand?" Most people, especially adults with low literacy skills, are likely to tell you they do understand the expressions even if they don't. They don't want to appear ignorant.

Decide which words simply must be understood. Make a short list and write a simple definition of each word in a conversational tone, and give an example of its use. Think of a question to ask to obtain feedback from the patient. Pretest the list with your patients. When you make your tape, include the definition right after the first use of the word to be defined.

Many nonmedical words can pose comprehension problems for patients and may need further explanation. This is especially true of adjectives and value judgment words. For example, a patient may be advised, "If your headache becomes severe, call me at once." The value judgment word, "severe", needs clarification. How severe? Severe for a moment or over several minutes? Clarification can take the form of specifics, with several examples, and, if appropriate, may be accompanied by demonstrations.

SUMMARY OF PRODUCTION STEPS

In summary, the following are the steps to produce an effective taped message:

---

gives over 300 words and definitions, at eighth- to ninth-grade levels.

1. Decide on purpose and scope. What is the desired behavior change?
2. List the relevant essential points to cover.
3. Consider the sequence of points to be covered.
4. Decide on feedback questions.
5. Break instruction into segments with a maximum duration of 5 to 10 minutes.
6. Record extemporaneously, **or** write the script in conversational tone; allow minor imperfections.
7. Pretest with a sample of your patient population (see Chap. 9).

TAPES AND RECORDER– PLAYER EQUIPMENT

In this section we will describe the recording equipment and tapes and how to select and use them.

For those without training in mechanical and electronic devices, tape players may present a confusing array of uncertainties. This section is intended to help you select and operate your tapes and recorder–players and to help you know what to do should things go wrong.

Battery-operated recorder–players are now available from more than a dozen manufacturers at prices under $40 (US). These recorders (Fig. 7-3) are simple to load and to operate.

Most recorder–players have five controls. Those with tab-like controls, like piano keys, as shown in Figure 7-3 are simplest to operate. The control functions usually are stop; play; record; rewind; and forward.

For patients, especially those with low literacy skills, it helps to color-code the controls by sticking a small round piece of paper or colored masking tape on the keys; red for stop; green for play; and yellow for rewind, or "get ready."

Battery-operated recorder–players offer the greatest flexibility for handling because they are portable, but battery life can become very short if the patient inadvertently leaves the control in the "on" position for long periods of time. For most situations where alternating current (AC) power is available, AC power is preferred over battery power.

Briefly test the recorder–player before purchase. Note

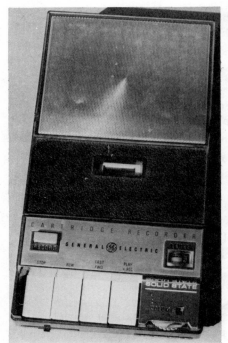

FIG. 7–3. Typical cassette recorder–player.

specifically the clarity of "s" sounds. If the "s" sounds hiss or whistle, don't buy the recorder–player.

To record your instruction, either a separate or built-in microphone can be used. Both types are available. When recording, place the microphone 10 to 20 inches away, and speak in a normal "meant-to-be-heard" conversational voice. If you hold the microphone too close, all the huffs and hisses made as you speak will be amplified. Record a brief trial message first, and then play it back to test for sound level. You may need to adjust either the distance or the sensitivity control.

Headphones provide privacy for the listener and reduce distractions from conversations and noise in the room. A headphone plug-in receptacle is included on most recorder-players so that either headphones or the built-in speaker can be used for listening.

Maintenance is fairly simple and is included in the instructions provided by the manufacturer. Usually the only maintenance needed is to clean the recorder–player head (the magnetic surfaces that contact the tape) with a cotton swab moistened with denatured alcohol every 100 hours or so of use. Remove the batteries if the unit is not to be used for several months.

If there is concern that the tape units are likely to be carried away, or the tapes removed, the unit can be secured by placing it within a lockable box so that only the control tabs are accessible. When purchasing recorder–players, look for those with built-in AC power converters. These units are the most troublefree.

SELECTION OF AUDIO TAPES

Buy the least expensive tapes you can find. Select 30-minute tapes, known as C-30, if you can find them. The longest tapes you should need are C-60, or 60-minute tapes, 30 minutes on each side. On sale, these are often available at much less than $1 per tape. High-fidelity tapes are not a requirement for voice recordings.

To make your recording on a tape cassette tamperproof, simply knock out the little tabs in the corners of the cassette (see Fig. 7-4). Holding the cassette with side A up, tape edge nearest to you, the tab on the left is for side "A", the one on the right for side "B." If later you wish to revise a tape, cover the knocked-out tab slots with cellophane tape.

One problem that is sometimes encountered after several playings is that the tape may become unevenly wound on the

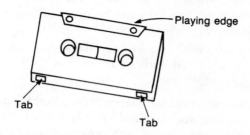

FIG. 7-4. *Knock-out tabs to make recording tamperproof.*

cassette spools. This condition causes increased friction, which usually slows down the tape speed so that the speech rate is abnormally slow. This condition can often be corrected by removing the cassette from the recorder–player and sharply rapping the cassette flat on a hard surface.

On rare occasions when handling a cassette, the tape may catch on some sharp object and pull out several feet of tape, leaving you with a tangle. If the tape is not broken or cut through, you can easily rewind it by inserting your little finger into the sprocket spool (either one) and rewinding in the direction that takes up the tape.

If the tape has been cut through, a temporary repair can be made with a small piece of cellophane tape. Carefully cut the tape ends so that they butt together evenly. Don't overlap the ends. Place the cellophane over the joint and trim the edges smoothly.

Audio tapes, like most typewriter ribbons, include a short leader piece at each end. Running time for the leader is typically 5 to 10 seconds. Nothing can be recorded during this time. When starting to record from the beginning of a tape, turn the take-up spool sprocket with your little finger until the colored leader tape is past. Then the tape is ready to record immediately.

SUMMARY

Choose audio tapes for instruction

- ☐ For visually impaired patients or when the patient prefers to listen
- ☐ For standardized or introductory instructions
- ☐ When there is a foreign language or dialect problem and the tape can be made in that language or dialect
- ☐ For adults with low literacy skills, especially when combined with a picture "book" or worksheet

We have seen that audio tapes carry a literacy demand, just as text does, but standardized, normed tests to determine comprehension level are not yet developed. Most commercially made tapes are difficult for patients with low literacy skills.

"Homemade" tapes can be far better. You can tailor your instruction to fit your patients at your location.

Planning includes the following: (1) select your objective in terms of desired change in patient behavior or skill; (2) select the relevant content and the sequence of presentation; (3) decide on dialog or monolog and then outline or write a script; (4) build in feedback questions; and (5) finally, pretest with your patients. Limit the message to 10 minutes. You can read from a script, but it is usually more natural and more effective if you record extemporaneously. Minor imperfections in the presentation are likely to help, rather than hinder, comprehension.

Inexpensive recorder–players are best; high-fidelity is not needed. Buy inexpensive tape cassettes; the C-30 and the C-60 are best.

Vocabulary learning, if kept to just a few words, can be included as a part of the instruction.

Tapes in combination with worksheets or picture books add learning reinforcement. For patients with low literacy skills, these methods can provide one of the least threatening learning environments.

REFERENCES

Brown JW, et al: Audio Materials. In AV Instruction, Technology, Media and Methods, 5th ed, p 201. New York, McGraw-Hill, 1977.

Doak LG, Doak CC: Patient comprehension profiles: Recent findings and strategies. Patient Counselling and Health Education 2, No. 3: 101–106, Winter, 1980

Kavanagh JF, Mattingly I: Language by Ear and by Eye: The Relationship Between Speech and Reading, Cambridge, MA, MIT Press, p 299, 1972

Sticht TG, et al. The Development of listening/looking and auding/reading processes, pp 45–70. In Auding and Reading: A Developmental Model. Human Research Resources Organization (HumRRO), Alexandria, VA, 1974 (Air Force Contract F41609-73-C-0025)

Sticht TG (ed): Reading for Working: A Functional Literacy Anthology, pp 98–104. Alexandria, VA, Human Research Resources Organization (HumRRO), 1975

Tuman MC: A comparative review of reading and listening comprehension. Journal of Reading 23, No. 8:702–703, May, 1980

CHAPTER EIGHT

Visuals and How to Use Them

There's more than what meets the eye when it comes to "reading" and understanding visuals. Reading a visual means interpreting the message the way the designer intended. You may not have associated the languaging process of text that we discussed in Chapter 2 with the learning from visuals, but comprehension of visuals depends on those same factors (i.e., the viewer's logic, language, and experience).

Most patient instruction carries a visual component in addition to prose or text. Photographs, sketches, cartoons, diagrams, and line-drawings, as well as demonstrations, all have a literacy demand. There are no "readability formulas" to determine the approximate capability required as we have for text, but, nonetheless, some visuals are much more understandable to adults with low literacy skills than are others. The objectives of this chapter are to present guidelines for visual perception and to explore the design of visuals that can effectively carry health messages to your patients.

Simplification is a critical requirement. This is one case where "less" is really "more." This point is especially true for adults with low literacy skills because you cannot rely on a title or caption to clarify a complex picture or to focus attention on the central theme. Visuals offer many advantages. They can reduce the amount of reading in the text; they can give emphasis to key points in your instruction; and they can motivate patients to use the instruction. Each of these advantages will be discussed along with notes of caution about the particular learning needs of patients.

We have drawn on a wide range of sources for the visuals presented in this chapter. All of them are appropriate in some settings, but some are less appropriate for adults with low literacy skills. In pointing out such distinctions, no criticism is intended or implied. Rather, these real-world case study examples are intended to contribute to your understanding of how visuals may be perceived by these patients.

Join us now in exploring visuals—and how they can make your health instructions more effective.

READING A VISUAL

Usually we think of "looking at" or "viewing" a visual, as we "view a show on TV." However, for health instruction purposes, we need to go beyond "looking" and focus attention on "reading." Visuals are indeed read very differently by different people. Many will give only one glance at a visual, and if they don't understand it right away, they will skip the page or stop reading the material altogether. Others may look at the visual at the wrong time during the instruction and so not understand its context. Still others will be captured by one detail and thus will miss the whole point of the visual.

Schramm and Roberts (1971) organized these reading behaviors to show how they may affect communication. The reading behaviors apply to both visuals and to text. They describe

□ **Selective exposure**—people choose to look at and read some content in preference to others.

□ **Selective perception**—people do not perceive all that is potentially available within whatever content or focus they have selected.

□ **Selective retention**—people do not retain or remember all of the information, the ideas, or the opinions they have perceived. This may be due to a faulty memory or because of repression or suppression.

The selectivities described by Schramm and Roberts correlate closely with observations made by the authors in teaching adults with low literacy skills. These people tend to scan and to comprehend very selectively.

These teaching observations also correlate with the work of Mackworth and Bruner (1970) who compared the ways that adults and children look at pictures. They found that adults who are poor readers are like children in that they are not systematic in scanning. They make a few long eye movements; their eyes wander about the picture in small steps; they often pass over the principal features. They lack precision in "aiming" and are slow in processing the perceptual information to arrive at the meaning of the picture.

We tend to see what we expect to see and not to see what is unexpected. An example of this, cited in a Peace Corps experience (Pett, 1976), describes a situation where a father, unfamiliar with photographs because of his remote rural life, could not recognize his own son in a photograph. The picture appeared simply as some grey shapes on white.

SOURCES OF VISUALS

Although most visuals being used in hospitals and in clinics were produced by commercial, government, or professional organizations, a surprising number of health-care professionals design and produce their own. In the Norfolk PHS hospital, 25% of the health instruction printed materials were produced by the hospital staff. Many of these were simple line-drawings. As we shall discuss later in this chapter, simple line-drawings are often more effective than any other format. Thus, local illustrators can produce effective visuals, and production costs for copies are lower than for more elaborate artwork.

PLANNING YOUR
USE OF VISUALS

In planning your use of visuals the most important concern is to narrow or limit the objective of what you want the patient to learn. Be very clear in your own mind why you are using a visual, and have only one or two purposes.

In Figure 8-1, the purpose appears to be a general one, perhaps of mood-setting, but the viewer is unsure of what to focus on. The title of the illustration in Figure 8-1 is "There are times when drinking and dreams don't mix."

The busy background in the illustration tends to confuse the adult with low literacy skills. Earlier, we discussed how the eye of the adult poor reader tends to wander over a page. In this case, where should the eye focus? On the woman's dress to

FIG. 8-1.   *A visual less appropriate for adults with low literacy skills. (Healthy Mothers, Healthy Babies Coalition. Washington, DC, Department of Health and Human Services, 1983)*

show pregnancy? Or on the baby on the moon? The key message about drinking is lost in the complexity of the illustration.

As an example of a specific illustration to show the purpose of instructional material, Figure 8-2, a title page for a

FIG. 8–2.   *Example of a visual more appropriate for adults with low literacy skills. (Swanson Center for Nutrition, Inc. 502 South 44th Street, Room 3007, Omaha, NE 68105, 1980)*

particular American Indian population, focuses the eye on the woman stirring the pot. The sketch of the woman is simple, direct, and life-like. The traditional Indian style adds interest as well as focusing attention. Those who can read the title would know that this material will help them understand that preparation of food affects the calories in a meal. The picture communicates a message that this material is likely to be about cooking.

By giving greater attention to the functions that visuals can serve, they can become much more than just decoration. They add variety and a dynamic quality to the page to greatly improve the instructional potential. We have discussed and emphasized the importance of repetition and drill for adults with low literacy skills, and visuals can keep interest up in this stage of instruction. They can help patients to remember information because pictures are often remembered better than words. They can help to jog the memory and to link new information with old knowledge.

There are many situations where visuals are especially suitable, either used in connection with oral instruction, with tapes, or with other forms of instruction. Some of those situations are

- ☐ When the patient prefers to learn by visual instruction
- ☐ For patients with impaired hearing
- ☐ For patients to understand steps in a procedure or the sequence of actions
- ☐ When there is a language difference
- ☐ To present introductory, routine, repetitive, or standardized instructions
- ☐ When the action to be taken can easily be visualized
- ☐ When combined with another instruction mode, such as tapes

WHY USE VISUALS?

We will discuss three reasons for using visuals to improve learning. There are other reasons, but the three discussed are most important for adults with low literacy skills. They are (1) to reduce the amount of reading in the text, (2) to give emphasis to your instruction, and (3) to provide motivation.

TO REDUCE READING IN THE TEXT

1. When You Want to Show Anatomical Relationships

When you find it necessary to use drawings of the anatomy of the body, be sure that you include enough in the drawings so that people can tell where the different structures or organs are located. The example in Figure 8-3 shows three ways of showing the breathing system.

When it is inappropriate to draw directly on a person as shown in the panel on the right in Figure 8-3, try to draw enough of the body to be sure that people can recognize what is shown. Include landmarks that people will recognize, and avoid cutting off arms and legs of patients. Compare the two illustrations of breech birth shown in Figure 8-4.

When the part of the anatomy is very small, try enlarging the view, still keeping the body part intact. In Figure 8-5, one half of the face was kept as an exterior view, the other half as an interior view. This drawing was used successfully in Alaska to teach Alaska Natives about otitis media.

LESS APPROPRIATE   MORE APPROPRIATE   STILL MORE APPROPRIATE

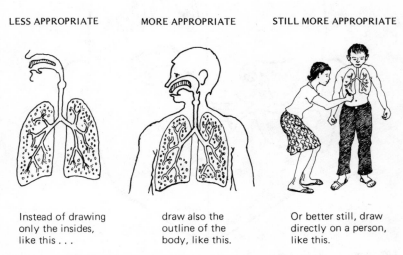

Instead of drawing only the insides, like this . . .

draw also the outline of the body, like this.

Or better still, draw directly on a person, like this.

FIG. 8-3.   *Select the appropriate way to show anatomy. (Werner D, Bower B: Helping Health Workers Learn, p 12-6. Palo Alto, The Hesperian Foundation, 1982)*

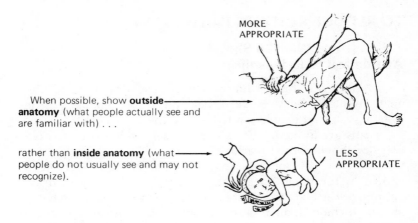

When possible, show **outside anatomy** (what people actually see and are familiar with) . . .

rather than **inside anatomy** (what people do not usually see and may not recognize).

MORE APPROPRIATE

LESS APPROPRIATE

FIG. 8–4.   *Show enough to ensure recognition. (Werner D, Bower B: Helping Health Workers Learn, p 12-7. Palo Alto, The Hesperian Foundation, 1982)*

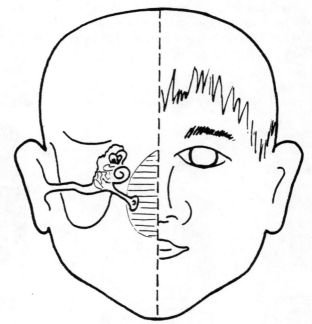

FIG. 8–5.   *Sample of enlargement of small part of anatomy—human face. Black-and-white line-drawing. Mastoid area on original was pink; middle and inner ear areas were green. (Left) Interior view. (Right) Exterior view. (McGrath Project, Division of Public Health, Department of Health and Welfare, Alaska, in cooperation with Children's Bureau, DHEW, 1962)*

2. When You Want to Describe Something Difficult to Put Into Words

One of the more difficult concepts to teach to nonreaders is the extreme smallness of microscopic organisms or cells. If a microscope is available, it helps to have patients use it to look at cells, such as malignant cells as compared with normal cells. If you are teaching about worm eggs or amebas, people who are literal minded have a hard time imagining that anything they can't see could possibly hurt them.

The presentations shown in Figures 8-6 and 8-7 are some

FIG. 8-6.   *Teaching the concept of magnification. (Werner D, Bower B: Helping Health Workers Learn, p 11-29. Palo Alto, The Hesperian Foundation, 1982)*

LESS APPROPRIATE

For example: The instructor here believes that this huge picture of a malaria mosquito will help students tell it apart from other mosquitoes. But the students do not recognize it as anything they have ever seen. The mosquitoes that bite them are not nearly so big or frightening.

THE BLACK FLY THAT SPREADS RIVER BLINDNESS LOOKS LIKE THIS:

BUT IT IS REALLY ONLY THIS BIG: ◄

MORE APPROPRIATE

Whenever oversized, bigger-than-life drawings are used, it is a good idea to include a small drawing of the thing showing its actual size.

STILL MORE APPROPRIATE

Even better than a drawing at actual size is, of course, to show the real thing—better alive than dead.

FIG. 8–7.   *Make sure your drawing communicates your message. (Werner D, Bower B: Helping Health Workers Learn, p 12-3. Palo Alto, The Hesperian Foundation, 1982)*

of the more imaginative approaches in teaching the concept of magnification (Werner and Bower, 1982). These ideas may also be helpful to you if you are teaching entry-level personnel who have no science background.

Making sure that your drawing communicates your message as clearly as possible suggests a caution at this point. Cartoon figures are often used to illustrate body parts or for physiological functions. Often the cartoon figures complicate the message by introducing a figure that is irrelevant to the message. For example, how might the adult with low literacy skills interpret the cartoon figure shown in Figure 8-8? Who is the man with brightly striped socks? Does he appear to be liquid like blood? Is food delivered on a tray? These are the kinds of perceptions generated in the minds of literal-minded people. Cartoons should be humanizing, should simplify, and should not add confusion to the message.

The blood that flows (circulates) through the body delivers the substances cells need

FIG. 8-8.   *Cartoon figures can confuse. (Feet First, A Booklet About Foot Care. Division of Nursing, Bureau of Health Manpower, PHS, US DHEW Pub. No. (HRA) 75-81)*

3. When You Need to Differentiate Sizes, Shapes, Positions for Exercises, and the Sequence of Actions

Often you may need to teach the proper size or shape of an object to a patient. This is one place where line drawings or photographs can be very useful. The example in Figure 8-9 is intended to show the relationship of the size of a pouch for an ostomy patient to the patient's height. The two figures in the illustration are intended to show short and tall people and where the pouch hangs relative to the groin.

The text provides additional information about the location of the ostomy, but the sketch carries the basic message.

Sketches and line drawings are very useful in teaching exercises for arthritis patients or for almost any kind of situation where body position is the focus of your instruction.

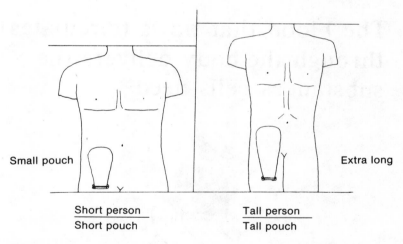

Small pouch

Extra long

Short person
Short pouch

Tall person
Tall pouch

FIG. 8-9. *Use illustrations to differentiate. (Home Health Care Center and Advisory Staff, University of Chicago Hospital and Clinics: Hints and Tips on Ostomy Care. Providence, RI, Davol, Inc, nd)*

The illustration needs to carry the message and should not be crowded on a page. The example shown in Figure 8-10, produced on one page of a 5- × 8-inch booklet, is clear to the reader and concentrates on the behavior to be followed.

There may be times when you need to teach a series of steps to be taken in a specific sequence. When you need to teach steps in a sequence, take care that the number of visuals does not overwhelm or confuse the poor reader. Rather than relying on arrows, lines, and similar directional instructions for the reader, place the visuals in sequence **along with the text** so that the eyes does not have to leave the sketch and travel someplace else to confirm what the message is. Adults with low literacy skills lose their place very easily when trying to follow a sequence of steps.

The following illustration shown in Figure 8-11 is a good example of providing a sequence of information, using a

Finger Exercises

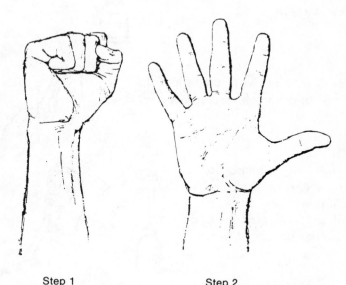

Step 1   Step 2

FIG. 8-10. *Making the illustration carry the message. (Simple Exercises for the Patient with Arthritis. National Institute of Arthritis, Metabolic, and Digestive Diseases, PHS, US DHEW, Arthritis Foundation. West Point, PA, Merck, Sharp, & Dohme, nd)*

ADMINISTRATION OF INSULIN

(Part of a sequence of steps)

SINGLE DOSE

1. Be sure hands are
    clean before starting.

2. Mix insulin by rolling bottle
    between the palms of the
    hands...DO NOT SHAKE...

3. Wipe rubber stopper
    on insulin bottle using
    an alcohol swab....

4. Fill syringe with air equal to
    the amount of insulin needed.

5. Push air into bottle,
    (prevents a vaccum
    inside the bottle)
    then turn syringe and
    bottle upside down....

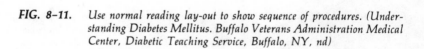

FIG. 8–11. *Use normal reading lay-out to show sequence of procedures. (Under-standing Diabetes Mellitus. Buffalo Veterans Administration Medical Center, Diabetic Teaching Service, Buffalo, NY, nd)*

combination of sketches and text. The eye travels in the usual left-to-right manner, down the page, and the captions or text are well placed in relation to the sketch. Notice that each step is numbered. The sketches are made in heavy black line drawings, and are presented with a consistent viewing angle to the reader. The sizes of the sketches are in proportion to one another.

TO GIVE EMPHASIS TO
YOUR INSTRUCTION

We have been discussing one major reason for using visuals, namely, to reduce the amount of reading in the text, and have provided several examples of situations when visuals are probably the most effective way to teach. Now let's consider other reasons for using visuals.

1. When You Want to Contrast
Normal and Abnormal Conditions,
Such as in Visual Acuity

It is important for the caption accompanying the visual to explain and identify the purpose of the visual. Sometimes we think that the picture or sketch can carry the entire message, but **when you are teaching contrasts,** the adult with low literacy skills must have the focus of the instruction **explained.** These captions in Figure 8-12 point out the contrasts between normal vision and the problem of restricted vision with glaucoma. If you cover up the captions, you might think that the first drawing represents daytime and the second represents night with a man carrying a flashlight.

In Figure 8-12, if you left the interpretation up to the reader and used a caption that said something like, "This is what happens to sight," the reader would not be sure what he was to look for in the illustration.

Sometimes emphasis is given by contrasting the right and the wrong way of carrying out an action. In such cases, the reader is often left to make the discriminations of what is "wrong" in the incorrect example as well as what is "right" in

Normal eyesight—this is how much you can see walking down the street when you have normal eyesight.

Glaucoma eyesight—notice how little you can see in front and around you when you have glaucoma. This is the same street scene as the one shown above in normal eyesight.

FIG. 8–12.   *Explain the visual: "Normal eyesight compared with glaucoma eyesight." (Glaucoma, the Sneak Thief of Sight. Prevention of Blindness Society of Metropolitan Washington, 1775 Church Street, N.W., Washington, DC, 20036)*

the correct one. This judgment is too much to ask of many readers who do not examine examples closely and who do not draw conclusions appropriately. Therefore, in using visuals to give emphasis to the correct way of carrying out a procedure or action, we recommend showing **only the right way.** This will avoid confusion and reduce the likelihood that the familiar way, often the wrong way, will be the one that is remembered. For example, in Figure 8-13, there are details that should be pointed

Turn your arm at the shoulder to open the jar.

Put the *palm* of your hand on the jar lid.

Put a wet towel under the jar to prevent sliding.

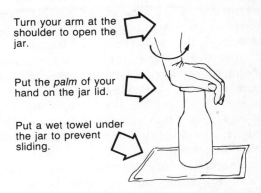

FIG. 8–13.   *Explanation of details that should be pointed out to the reader. Explain the visual: "Protect your fingers by opening a jar with your arm and your hand." (Joint Protection Techniques for Rheumatoid Arthritis Patients. Pittsburgh, St. Margaret Memorial Hospital)*

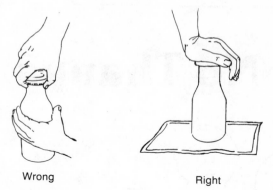

Wrong   Right

FIG. 8–14.   *Example of a wrong and a right way to open a screw-top jar, shown together without detailed captions. (Joint Protection Techniques for Rheumatoid Arthritis Patients. Pittsburgh, St. Margaret Memorial Hospital)*

out to the reader for the correct way for opening a screw-top jar to give adequate finger joint protection.

If you show the wrong and the right way, and if you do not use captions to point out the details of the correct way, the adult with low literacy skills may remember what he knows. It may be the incorrect way. Even though the information may be in the text, he can easily miss it.

This is an example of a wrong and a right way, shown together without detailed captions (Fig. 8-14). The explanation is in the text.

2. When You Want to Dramatize the Behavior

Sometimes the message needs to be dramatized to show its importance as well as to communicate how a patient can carry out the instruction. For example, in weight-control programs, cutting out desserts and sweets in a social setting may be very difficult for some patients. The line-drawing in Figure 8-15 indicates the behavior expected of the viewer and has no distracting background. Notice that the figures have eyes, mouths, noses, ears, and a facial expression, giving them a human feeling. When you use simple line-drawings, make people look as human as possible.

FIG. 8–15.   *Simple figures communicate best. This example indicates the behavior expected and has no distracting background. (Developed for the Healthy People Project by Nutrition Services and the Health Education Center, Maryland Department of Health and Mental Hygiene, Baltimore, MD, 1982, and funded by CDC Grant No. H-11/CCH-300-327-03-1)*

The drawing in Figure 8-15 is intended to help the patient counting calories to refuse friendly offers of desserts at a party. It is one in a series of instructions on weight control for a flip chart presentation.

It is important to have the visual show the behavior you want by reinforcing the message. The photograph in Figure 8-16 illustrates the behavior desired, reinforced by the action title, which is placed right next to the photograph.

You may want to give emphasis by dramatizing the "call to action" as the summary or at the end of a brochure. The illustration in Figure 8-17 is used at the conclusion of a multi-

THE SOONER YOU QUIT SMOKING THE BETTER

FIG. 8–16. *Use visuals to show desired behavior change. (I Quit Smoking Because I Love My Baby. New York, American Lung Association, 1982)*

FIG. 8–17. *Use visuals for a "call to action." (VD! Std! or What? Health Promotion and Education Office, Hawaii State Department of Health, Honolulu, Hawaii, 1982)*

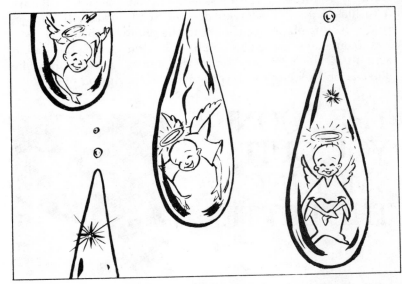

FIG. 8–18.   *Will patients understand the desired behavior from this visual? It might be more useful to show several views of a clock and a patient taking eye drops than to emphasize "goodness" by using angel figures. (Glaucoma, the Sneak Thief of Sight. Prevention of Blindness Society of Metropolitan Washington, 1775 Church Street, NW, Washington, DC 20036)*

page brochure on venereal disease. The message is printed in lower-case letters (easy for poor readers), the sketch illustrates the behavior expected, and the caption ties in directly with the visual. By showing a person using the telephone to call the clinic, the viewer is encouraged and there is reinforcement to take action.

It is indeed a difficult task to teach patients to use any kind of medication regularly. A number of different kinds of devices are employed to help establish medication habit patterns. Visuals are often used to dramatize the importance of regular habits, but sometimes the visual can interfere with the message. For example, in Figure 8-18, some patients would have a difficult time associating the "good" exemplified by the angel in the eye drop with what they normally think of as an eye drop.

3. For Specific Information

There are times when you may wish to direct attention to the critical information in text or in reading labels or in drug information. Cues such as circles, arrows, larger print, color, or underlining are useful in helping the eye focus on the relevant information. Figure 8-19 is an example of how critical cues are

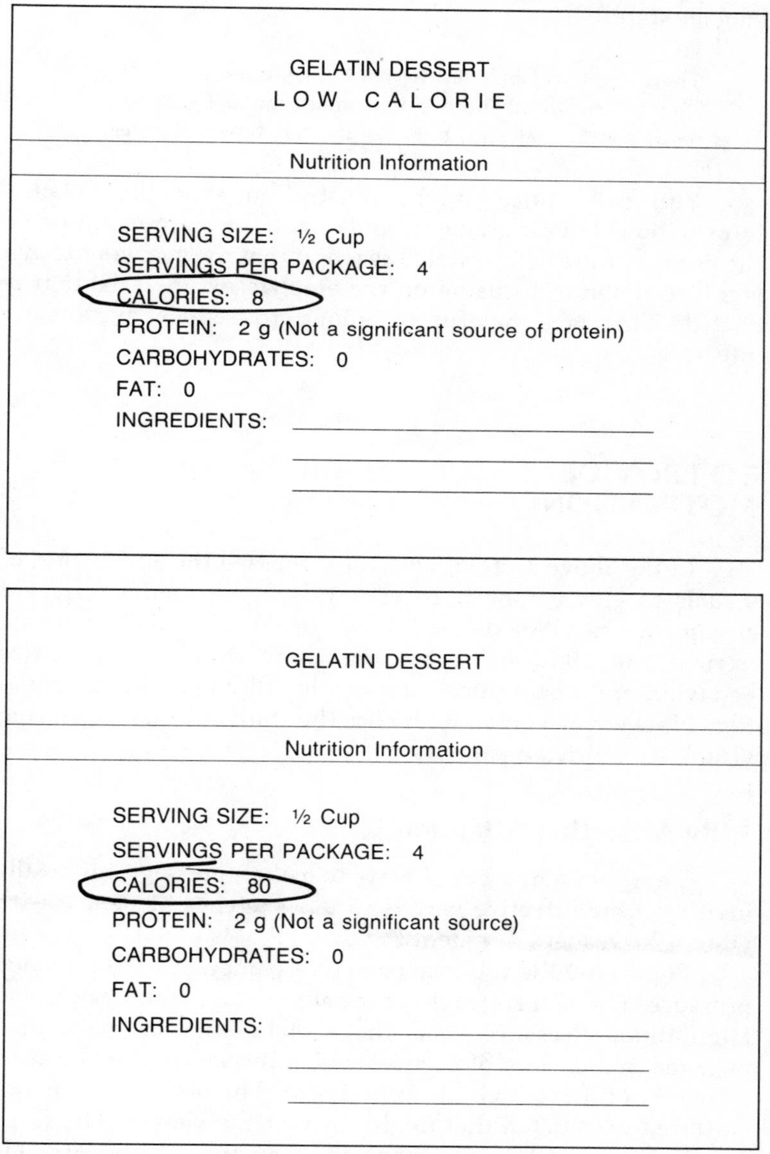

GELATIN DESSERT
L O W   C A L O R I E

Nutrition Information

SERVING SIZE: ½ Cup
SERVINGS PER PACKAGE: 4
CALORIES: 8
PROTEIN: 2 g (Not a significant source of protein)
CARBOHYDRATES: 0
FAT: 0
INGREDIENTS: _____
_____
_____

GELATIN DESSERT

Nutrition Information

SERVING SIZE: ½ Cup
SERVINGS PER PACKAGE: 4
CALORIES: 80
PROTEIN: 2 g (Not a significant source)
CARBOHYDRATES: 0
FAT: 0
INGREDIENTS: _____
_____
_____

FIG. 8-19.   *Using emphasis to show difference or key point. (Eat Less Sugar, Swanson Center for Nutrition, Inc, 502 South 44th Street, Room 3007, Omaha, NE 68105, 1980)*

employed in a nutrition instruction booklet to teach patients how to read labels for low calorie foods. The instruction in the booklet states:

> There are two labels on the next page. One is from a "low calorie" food and one is from a regular food. Both foods contain calories, but one just has **fewer calories.**

You will notice in the illustration that the detailed information about ingredients and directions on preparation of the product were deliberately fuzzed so that the eye would have less distraction in focusing on the emphasized material that is circled. This is a helpful technique to reduce extraneous interference.

TO PROVIDE MOTIVATION

In the above section, we have discussed the advantages of visuals to give emphasis to your instruction under different circumstances. We showed how visuals can help contrast normal and abnormal conditions, how they can dramatize behavior, and how critical cues can highlight specific information. Now we will go on to discuss the third advantage of using visuals, to motivate patients.

1. By Attracting Attention

There are a number of ways to make a message personally inviting. One effective way is to use sketches of people with whom the readers can identify.

Figure 8-20 is the title page of a pamphlet on high blood pressure. The text states that the pamphlet is about "Blacks and High Blood Pressure" and the sketches are of black men engaged in a variety of occupations, inferring that you can be active if you have high blood pressure. The background is not cluttered with detail that might distract the viewer. The facial expressions are pleasant, giving the viewer a positive attitude and creating a more dynamic feeling than words could convey.

FIG. 8-20.   *Sample of visual to identify and attract attention. (US Department of Health and Human Services, Public Health Service, National Institutes of Health)*

Devices to attract attention are more limited in levels of sophistication for poor readers than for good readers. The logic and experience backgrounds of poor readers are not as varied, and abstractions in art forms are not often part of their comprehension. For example, stylized drawings are usually simplified so much that the personal quality is lost.

Figure 8-21 is the title page of a pamphlet designed for low-income women (WIC is the acronym for the federal food supplement program for Women, Infants, and Children). Unfortunately, the symbol of a woman and her children is stylized

WIC
FOODS
HELP!

CHEESE

FIG. 8–21.   *Avoid using stylized visuals. (Department of Human Services, Commission of Public Health, WIC Program, 1873 Connecticut Avenue, Room 830-E, Washington, DC 20009. Credit WIC Program, Virginia Department of Health, nd)*

and the interpretation tends to be either puzzlement or "that's not me."

Animals or fish are sometimes used to attract attention. If you decide to use this device, try to make the animal or fish relevant to the message. Figure 8-22 is a cover on an excellent brochure on chronic obstructive pulmonary disease (COPD). The crab has a name, "Snappy," and is used throughout the booklet. However, the crab bears no relationship to the subject, nor to the reader. The crab may be a local attraction in a fishing community, but even so it stretches the imagination so far that the seriousness of COPD may seem far-fetched.

Another effective way of attracting attention for poor readers is to use a story-telling approach. Comic books offer an exciting way for helping these readers not only to identify with the characters in the story, but also to learn the message in a context that they can understand.

Werner and Bower (1982) point out that in many countries, especially in Latin America, people read comic books more

FIG. 8-22.   *Example of a poor visual for adults with low literacy skills. Attention-getting devices can be irrelevant.*

than any other written material. They have found that people will find stories more real and more interesting if the characters have names instead of just "this boy," "that baby," or "those people." The story should seem as life-like as possible. Keep the messages short, with not more than fifteen words in a "balloon." Use lower-case rather than all capital letters.

In Figure 8-23, Rex Morgan, M.D., is the principal character. Readers who follow the comics in the newspapers would quickly recognize him. However, many poor readers do not read the newspapers regularly. Therefore, in thinking about designing a comic book series, pretest your draft material with a sample of your patient population. Pretest for the format of comic books to see if your population does read in sequence easily (Pett, 1976) and that the theme and the characters are quickly recognized. You may need to compose your own stories to fit your particular population (Werner and Bower, 1982).

FIG. 8-23. *Comic book story adds interest for many readers. (Rex Morgan, M.D., Talks About Your Unborn Child. National Clearinghouse for Alcohol Information (NCALI), Department ATF-FAS, PO Box 2345, Rockville, MD 20852, nd)*

However, the payoff in terms of motivating your particular patient population may well be worth all the effort.

Another significant factor in attracting attention is finding a meaningful life-style in the picture. A life-style that is familiar and desirable helps in establishing credibility. Conversely, a life-style that is too sophisticated may turn adults with low literacy skills away from the message entirely. For example, one teaching brochure, *How to Take Insulin,* shows a young person in a bathroom that is done in decorator colors and has fixtures of the highest quality. The setting is fashionable and expensive. But a number of health professionals said that they could not use this material with their patients because their patients did not have bathrooms like that. Their patients were at a poverty level. The photograph lacked credibility for these patients and prevented their serious interest in the contents despite excellent technical photographs. Conversely, this illustration may have high credibility for upper middle class patients who can identify with the person in this sophisticated setting.

2. By Adding Variety and Breaks in the Text

Many patient education materials contain lists of information that the reader is expected to use in making decisions. Sometimes there are lists of symptoms such as the "seven danger signals of cancer," or symptoms of the onset of illness, or of foods on diets.

Lists present a problem in comprehension for adults with low literacy skills who may begin to lose track of the subject as they move down the page and encounter new information as they go. If their eyes move back up to the title of the list to reconfirm what this list is all about, there is a good chance that they will lose their place when they return to the body of the list or text. When they lose their place, they may become frustrated, bored, or annoyed to the point of ignoring the whole message.

One way to address this problem is by adding variety through the use of visuals, which also helps in breaking a long line of text. Notice Figures 8-24 and 8-25. The focus in these illustrations is just on the foods, **not on food and amounts simultaneously.** The aspect of the food given emphasis is the tactile quality: how does it feel, how does it taste, and what is its consistency? These are the ways people perceive and

Different foods and beverages have different amounts of calories.

If a food is:

— Oily or greasy-crisp . . . . like fried potatoes, fried bread, fried chicken

— Smooth, slick, or greasy . . . . like mayonnaise, salad dressings, oils, margarine

— Smooth, sweet or sticky . . . . like malt, syrup, candy, pop, pop-sicles, ice cream

— Contains alcohol . . . . like beer, wine, whiskey

Then it is probably high in calories.

FIG. 8–24. *Sample illustration showing the effective use of variety to add interest to a long line of text. (Eat Less Food, p. 8. Swanson Center for Nutrition, Inc, Omaha, NE, 1980)*

If a food is:

— Bulky or has lots of fiber or coarseness . . . like apple, broccoli, cabbage, green beans, whole wheat bread

— Thin and watery . . . like coffee, tea, water, diet drinks

— Water-crisp rather than greasy-crisp . . . like celery, carrots, lettuce, cauliflower.

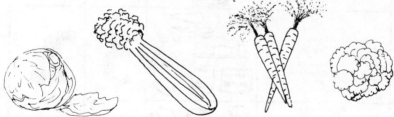

Then it is probably low in calories

FIG. 8–25. *Sample illustration that adds interest through variety of visuals as well as showing food categories. (Eat Less Food, p. 9. Swanson Center for Nutrition, Inc, Omaha, NE, 1980)*

recognize food. Linking these qualities with caloric information helps to simplify the point. Rich foods or alcoholic beverages are probably high in calories whereas the bulky, watery, or water-crisp foods have few calories.

The problems of providing for patient choice of foods, amount of foods, number of servings, and differing patient conditions on a single visual are considerable. In the example shown in Figure 8-26, the pregnant patient is provided with a list for guidance in deciding how many servings from a given food group should be eaten every day, depending on her pre- or postpartum condition. The difficulty in the illustration shown in Figure 8-26 is that the list, the illustrations, and the two sets of numbers on the right side all have to be seen in relation to each other in order to be comprehended. Most adults with low literacy skills do not have experience in organizing information in this manner.

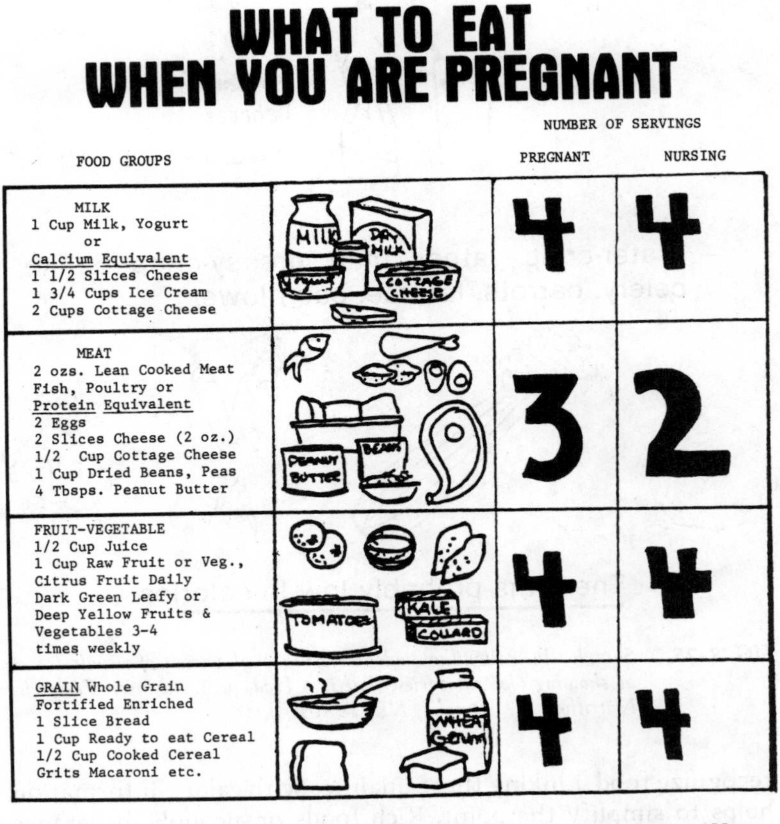

WHAT TO EAT
WHEN YOU ARE PREGNANT

| | | NUMBER OF SERVINGS | |
FOOD GROUPS		PREGNANT	NURSING
MILK 1 Cup Milk, Yogurt or Calcium Equivalent 1 1/2 Slices Cheese 1 3/4 Cups Ice Cream 2 Cups Cottage Cheese		4	4
MEAT 2 ozs. Lean Cooked Meat Fish, Poultry or Protein Equivalent 2 Eggs 2 Slices Cheese (2 oz.) 1/2 Cup Cottage Cheese 1 Cup Dried Beans, Peas 4 Tbsps. Peanut Butter		3	2
FRUIT-VEGETABLE 1/2 Cup Juice 1 Cup Raw Fruit or Veg., Citrus Fruit Daily Dark Green Leafy or Deep Yellow Fruits & Vegetables 3-4 times weekly		4	4
GRAIN Whole Grain Fortified Enriched 1 Slice Bread 1 Cup Ready to eat Cereal 1/2 Cup Cooked Cereal Grits Macaroni etc.		4	4

FIG. 8-26. *Avoid overloaded visuals. (District of Columbia, Department of Human Resources, Commodity Supplemental Food Branch, May, 1979)*

In this section, we have discussed the advantages of visuals to provide motivation for patients by attracting their attention through the use of sketches of people with whom the readers can identify. Through the use of stories in a comic book format readers can become interested and concerned about the message being presented. Using the patients' life-style, readers can identify with the environment and establish credibility. Visuals can help make lists of information more understandable.

TIPS TO IMPROVE YOUR VISUALS FOR POOR READERS

Captions and Titles

A caption or title is needed to relate most illustrations to the text. But captions do much more, such as pointing out the essential message or theme of the illustration. Thus, the caption preconditions the readers as to what to look for and how to understand the author's message.

Action captions not only help the reader understand but also direct the reader toward what to do. For example, an illustration with three alternative captions that range from less to most appropriate is shown in Figure 8-27.

Brevity is essential for most captions; try to stay within ten words. An exception would be a pictorial sequence where

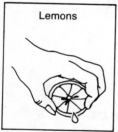
A. Less appropriate

B. More appropriate

C. Most appropriate

FIG. 8–27.   *Sample illustration of action captions within a figure to improve effectiveness. (Adapted from instructional material prepared by Nutrition Services, Administration for Services to Chronically Ill and Aging, Maryland Department of Health and Mental Hygiene, Baltimore, MD and funded by NHLBI Contract No. 1-HV-7-2986, 1981)*

step-by-step procedures are required, such as in insulin administration or for some types of exercises.

Good captions, like good newspaper headlines, take a little
time to create. A good starting place is to decide on the one
essential behavior your message is intended to convey. Then
use an action verb in a short telegram-like caption. Pretest the
caption and illustration with patients.

Illustrations and captions should be consistent in their
message. Both the captions and the illustration should emphasize the correct behavior and should avoid the possibility of the
reader getting the wrong message. For example, in Figure 8-28,
the child is doing what the first caption says, which is negative.
The advice to parents is in very small print and is not shown in
the illustration.

**YOUNG CHILDREN WILL EAT AND DRINK
ALMOST ANYTHING!**

Keep all liquids and solids that may be poisonous
out of their reach.

FIG. 8-28.   *Example of a poor visual for adults with low literacy skills. Avoid
illustrations and captions that cite incorrect behavior. (Poison Prevention
Week Council)*

Color

The use of color often comes up in the design of materials. As a general guideline, except for the rare occasion where a color photograph is necessary, use the fewest colors consistent with the essential message of the visual. An example of color for learning is in teaching color differentiation for urine-testing.

Multicolor visuals are frequently used in teaching nutrition to portray foods and possibly to attract the readers' attention. But in almost all cases simple black-and-white line-drawings that show shape and texture would be as suitable and less expensive. They might also be preferable to poor readers. Increasing the number of colors will often make no improvement in comprehension, but it certainly will increase the cost.

If multicolor illustrations are planned, the fewest possible number of colors should be used. Consistency should be maintained in the meaning of each color from one illustration to the next. Dwyer (1971) has found that color can be an effective typographic cue if used sparingly and if its function is explained, or is obvious, to the reader.

Some colors are preferred for clarity. Traffic signs are usually black printing on a yellow background because this color combination provides the best contrast for most people. Yellow printing on a black background is also very good for contrast. Black printing on a white background is easy to read. However, when white printing is used on a black background, there is a 10% reduction in reading speed (Paterson and Tinker, 1931). As the contrast between background and print is decreased, speed of perception is reduced.

Remember that many people will be reading your instruction materials under poor lighting conditions. This means that sharp contrasts are preferable for ease in reading. Beige print on beige paper or pale greens, pinks, and blues are difficult to read even under good lighting conditions.

Lay-out and Camera Angles

Use lots of white space to reduce eye distraction for poor readers. One step of a procedure should be presented at one time and on one page so that the reader can understand the step without having to turn the page.

If you are presenting a series of steps such as those shown in Figure 8-11 on insulin administration, place the captions and the drawings in the left-to-right order and down the page in the normal reading order. Avoid using a matrix design of only drawings or photographs such as the design shown in Figure 8-29. In this illustration the reader doesn't know in which direction he should read and his eyes can travel around the page without a sense of order or sequence.

Photographs and drawings should be taken from the user's viewpoint, again as shown in Figure 8-11. Do not change the camera or viewing angle unless critical cues can be observed only from other angles. In such cases, indicate by dotted lines or arrows what changes have been made. Otherwise you may lose the reader.

Photographs or Line-Drawings?

There seems to be a traditional belief that realistic visual formats, such as photographs and detailed drawings, are generally more effective than are less realistic formats. However, Dwyer (1972) found that the effectiveness was related to the amount of time available for viewing. He found that realistic photographs were more effective when the learner was able to control the amount of viewing time, whereas line-drawings were more effective when the viewing time was controlled, as in television and slide-tape presentations. In our opinion, the Figure 8-30 summarizes the pros and cons of different kinds of illustrations.

Typography

Throughout this book we have pointed out the need for lower-case type for poor readers. They need the differentiation of "humps and bumps" and the above and below the line characteristics of lower case letters in order to recognize them.

Adults use the distinguishing features of letters just as

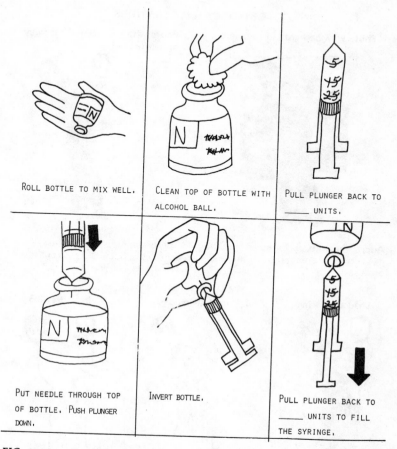

ROLL BOTTLE TO MIX WELL.

CLEAN TOP OF BOTTLE WITH ALCOHOL BALL.

PULL PLUNGER BACK TO _____ UNITS.

PUT NEEDLE THROUGH TOP OF BOTTLE. PUSH PLUNGER DOWN.

INVERT BOTTLE.

PULL PLUNGER BACK TO _____ UNITS TO FILL THE SYRINGE.

FIG. 8–29. *Example of poor illustration for adults with low literacy skills. Avoid unnumbered matrix visuals.*

children do (Gibson et al, 1968). We take into account curved versus straight lines; diagonal versus horizontal lines; intersecting lines; and closed versus open curves to get the cues that rapid decoding require. Diagonal lines are more difficult; poor readers tend to confuse letters, such as *M* with *N* and *M* with *W*; capital letters all fit within a box. They lack the ascending and descending characteristics of lower-case letters. Because there are fewer distinctive cues, all capitals or upper-case letters are more difficult to read.

FIVE KINDS OF ILLUSTRATIONS

1. Photo with background complete

Appropriate if background adds to the message (but here it adds nothing and confuses).

2. Photo with background cut away or 'whited out'

Appropriate for many health illustrations. Subject stands out more clearly. Less confusing.

3. Shaded drawing

Usually less appropriate because it is difficult for people to copy and because heavy shadows can be confusing. (People might wonder, "Why is the baby's neck black?")

4. Line drawing

Often most appropriate because it is relatively simple, yet adequately detailed. Relatively easy for people to copy for flip charts or posters.

5. Stylized drawing

Usually less appropriate. Simplified so much that personal quality is lost. People will not identify as much with these characters.

FIG. 8-30.   *Drawings are more effective for adults with low literacy skills. (Abbatt FR: Teaching for Better Learning. World Health Organization, 1980)*

For emphasis, <u>underline</u> rather than change type style from lower-case letters to all capitals. In the following example, it would have been better to underline rather than switch to all capitals:

Do NOT add sugar

Many patients with low literacy skills cannot read script although they may be able to read lower-case typed words. We therefore recommend that you **not** use *italics* or script on your typewriter when you are preparing material for these people.

The width of a line seems to be best when typed in two columns on a page. These lines are neither too short nor too long. The short line results in longer eye fixations on it, which helps comprehension; the longer line results in eye difficulty on the return sweep to the next line (Paterson and Tinker, 1940).

In selecting size of type, we recommend the larger point type, preferably 14 point. The following examples show a range of type sizes:

This is a sample of the 8 point type.

This is a sample of the 10 point type.

This is a sample of the 12 point type.

This is a sample of the 14 point type.

This is a sample of the 18 point type.

Avoid fancy typefaces. For example, Tinker and Paterson (1941) found, through eye movement photographs, that Old English typeface "reduced the span of perception, increased the number of eye fixations as well as the total perception time, and the number of regressive movements." Comprehension suffered.

The following are examples of shaded letters and stylized typefaces that are difficult for poor readers to comprehend:

CALL THE HOSPITAL

DRUGS

Symbols may be difficult for poor readers. They may stop and try to figure them out, and then their attention shifts from the message over the symbols (Fig. 8-31). Use words such as "add" instead of "+" and "equals" instead of "=".

PICTOGRAPHS

Statistical data are confusing for many very literate people. They are especially confusing for adults with low literacy skills because their universe tends to be more restricted to their immediate surroundings and they are unconcerned about whether statistically they are one in ten or one in a thousand. Figure 8-32 shows how statistical data can be presented in pictographs.

Pictographs often confuse adults with low literacy skills. It doesn't really matter how the data are presented because the *concept* will almost surely be too abstract. That there are "lots" of other people like them is about as far as you need to go in explaining the statistics of their condition.

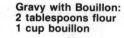

Gravy with Bouillon:
2 tablespoons flour
1 cup bouillon

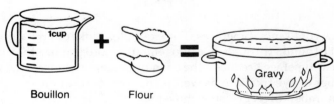

FIG. 8–31.   *An example of a poor visual for adults with low literacy skills. Avoid using symbols because they can confuse poor readers. (Swanson Center for Nutrition, Inc. Food Preparation Affects Calories, p 9. Omaha, NE, 1980)*

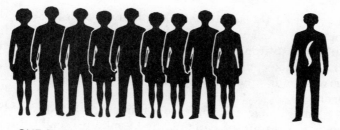

ONE OUT OF TEN AFRO-AMERICANS CARRIES THE GENE

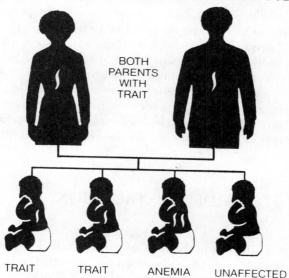

BOTH
PARENTS
WITH
TRAIT

TRAIT   TRAIT   ANEMIA   UNAFFECTED

Statistical data on Sickle Cell Anemia

FIG. 8–32.   *A sample of a poor illustration for adults with low literacy skills. Avoid using pictographs for visuals because they are often confusing. (Sickle Cell Anemia, Public Health Education Information Sheet. March of Dimes Birth Defects Foundation, 1275 Mamaroneck Avenue, White Plains, NY 10605)*

FILMS, FILM STRIPS, AND SLIDES

Films, film strips, and slides carry a powerful potential for learning. Most of the films and film strips are produced either by professional organizations or through government or commercial sources. There are very few of these visual forms that are produced for adults with low literacy skills, so for these people you probably need to change your way of using films. You'll need to stop after two or so concepts have been presented rather than keeping the film running through its entirety. The overwhelming amount of information can greatly reduce the learning.

For example, we observed a film strip on foot care being shown to a group of patients. In 11 minutes, eight different concepts had been presented, about one every 75 seconds. That is mind-boggling for the poor reader. For these people, it is more effective to stop the film every few minutes, turn on the lights, and conduct a discussion with the patients on what they have just seen and heard (most are sound films and film strips).

Introduce vocabulary before the film is shown. If there is animation in the film, it is better to cue the audience in ahead of time than merely to show the film and hope they can figure out what's going on. Animation is often used by film producers to keep interest up, and it may or may not be relevant to the health message.

COMPUTER-AIDED INSTRUCTION

Can the adult with low literacy skills use programmed instruction? The comprehension of the message depends on the same factors that we have discussed throughout the book. The added problem may be the access to the message. If the equipment is complicated or requires keyboard knowledge or other implementation devices, the novelty of the technology rather than the health message may receive the person's attention.

There are advantages to the use of computer-aided instruction if the equipment does not present a problem. It offers standardized information, can be reviewed and repeated many times without change in presentation or tone, and is usually available when the patient needs the information.

SUMMARY

Visuals help reduce the burden of many details in the text. They give emphasis to important points, and they motivate the users to read the material. They aid comprehension by adding another dimension when words alone are insufficient to get the message across.

Effectiveness is directly related to how well the illustration fits the message. People perceive the illustration based on their own experience. Since we seldom can walk in the other person's shoes, it is important to pretest visuals with a sample of your intended population.

Visuals should be simple, should contain only one or two messages, and should be as free from clutter and distraction as possible. Eye movements of persons with low literacy skills are not as disciplined nor as educated as those of good readers, so that placement of the visual and ample white space are important factors for comprehension.

Cues as to what to look for are important aids for adults with low literacy skills in order for them to understand the message you intend. Circles, arrows, and other devices help to draw attention to critical information.

Use adult concepts rather than childish animation to stimulate interest. When using sketches, drawings, and cartoons, make the figures resemble humans as closely as possible.

REFERENCES

Dwyer F: Color as an instructional variable. Audio Visual Communication Review 19:399–416, 1971. As quoted in Document Design: A Review of the Relevant Research, Felker DB (ed): Washington, DC, American Institutes for Research, 1980 pp 104–106

Dwyer FM: A Guide for Improving Visualized Instruction. State College, PA, Learning Services, 1972. As quoted in Jonassen DH: The Technology of Text: Principles for Structuring, Designing, and Displaying Text, p 308. Englewood Cliffs, NJ, Educational Technology Publications, 1982

Gibson EJ, Schapiro F, Yonas A: Confusion matrices for graphic patterns obtained with a latency measure. In Levin H, Gibson EJ, Gibson JJ (eds): The Analysis of Reading Skill. Final Report, Project No. 5-1213, U.S. Dept. of Health, Education, and Welfare, 1968. As quoted in Vernon MD: Visual Perception and Its Relation to Reading, p 12. Newark, DE, International Reading Association, 1973

Mackworth NS, Bruner JS: How adults and children search and recognize pictures. Human Development 13:149–158, 1970. As quoted in Vernon MD: Visual Perception and its Relation to

Reading, p 5. Newark, DE, International Reading Association, 1973

Paterson DG, Tinker MA: Studies of typographical factors influencing speed of reading. Journal of Applied Psychology 15:241–247, 1931. As quoted in Berger A, Peebles JD: Rates of Comprehension, p 26. International Reading Association, Newark DE, 1976

Paterson DG, Tinker MA: Influences of line width on eye movements. Journal of Experimental Psychology 27:572–577, 1940. As quoted in Berger A, Peebles JD: Rates of Comprehension, p 27. Newark, DE, International Reading Association, 1976

Pett DW: Audio-Visual Communication Handbook, p 4. Peace Corps Contract 25-1707 with Audio Visual Center, Indiana University, Bloomington, Indiana. Published by World Neighbors, 5116 No. Portland Avenue, Oklahoma City, OK, 73112, 1976

Schramm W, Roberts D (eds): The Process and Effects of Mass Communication. Urbana, IL, University of Illinois Press, 1971. As quoted in Hicks RC: A Survey of Mass Communication, p 306. Gretna, LA, Pelican Publishing, 1977

Tinker MA, Paterson DG: Eye movements in reading a modern typeface and Old English. American Journal of Psychology 54:113–114, 1941. As quoted in Berger A, Peebles JD: Rates of Comprehension, p 29. Newark, DE, International Reading Association, 1976

Werner D. Bower B: Helping Health Workers Learn, pp 11-29; 12-3. Palo Alto, CA, The Hesperian Foundation, 1982

Ibid, 1982, p 13-10, 11

CHAPTER NINE

Pretesting

Let's suppose you have your written, visual, or audio tape instruction drafted, and it has been checked for its scientific accuracy. Further, you've done a readability measurement and you're satisfied that it is at a level that will communicate with your audience. Are you ready for production and distribution? Not quite yet. Instructional material needs to be pretested with the prospective user before it is ready for wider distribution, even within your own clinical setting. Although patients may be able to read the words or listen to the tapes, you need to test to determine if the concepts are coming through the way you intend.

Testing is needed even with visuals. You just can't predict how people will interpret your well-intentioned messages. One nurse pretested a series of sketches on urine testing for diabetes. It seemed to be a straightforward series showing a person drinking water in the morning and then carrying out urine-testing procedures. But not everybody understood. One patient perceived the sketches differently. He said, "You mean I have to drink my urine to test it?" Sketches need captions.

This chapter defines and identifies the components of pretesting, describes the procedures, discusses possible stages of production for pretesting along the way, and provides some examples of the results of pretesting.

WHAT IS PRETESTING?

Pretesting is a systematic way of finding out if your message is coming across to the users with the meaning that you intended it to have. It identifies elements in the communication that could be changed to make it more effective. Sometimes its purpose is to determine systematically which of several alternative versions of a communication will work best.

145

WHAT ARE THE CRITICAL COMPONENTS OF PRETESTING? (Bertrand, 1978)

Attraction

First, you want a persuasive communication to be attractive to the patient. Is the message interesting enough to attract and hold the attention of the target audience? If it is a visual, is the picture pleasing to the target audience? Are the colors clear? If it is a tape, is the voice pleasing? Diction distinct? Speed reasonable? Does the voice have an accent acceptable to the locality?

Comprehension

Two of the most critical components for patients with low literacy skills are comprehension and interest. Can the patients tell you in their own words what the message is? What other interpretations are possible? Are there so many actions that patients become confused? (Remember the drinking of water and the urine-testing message.) Have you used general terms that may not mean to patients what they mean to you?

Demonstration

Can patients demonstrate for you what they are to do as a result of being exposed to the message? Comprehension occurs when the receiver can transform the message from one format to another. Thus, if patients read or listen they should be able to restate the message in their own words or show you through demonstration what the message says.

Self-involvement

Do patients feel that the message is **for them** as individuals, not directed to a mass of people who may have the same problem? Are there elements such as a wine glass or modern furniture or other features in the communication that may distract from the message or make it too sophisticated for your audience?

Acceptability

Is the message in any way offensive? Sometimes cartoons show body cells as little men. This may be an artist's delight, but humor can make the message seem unimportant and therefore the patient may ignore it. This is a particular point to test out with patients with low literacy skills. Is the message perceived by the patient as true? Are there any annoying elements? Our value systems, especially when it comes to humor, may not be perceived the same way by others. Humor and ridicule can be very similar. A physician portrayed with a headband supporting a light looked like a coal miner to some patients. Therefore, even the way health professionals are shown needs to be pretested.

Persuasion

Is the message able to convince people that they should take action? An instructional message, even a very good one, is unlikely to induce behavior change all by itself. Nonetheless, the message should be as persuasive as you can make it.

WHAT ARE THE PROCEDURES FOR PRETESTING?

The design of any pretest has to be individually tailored to the type of communication being tested. Although there is no standard formula for pretesting, there are guidelines to help you. We'll discuss these guidelines in the context of different media.

Written Text

If you are pretesting material such as a set of eight or ten specific instructions, identify the words or phrases in the instruction that are the keys to the comprehension of the message (we give an example of this point later in this chapter). Ask the patient to tell you what these words mean to him. If your patient has less than a fifth-grade reading ability, or if you have serious doubts about his reading ability, read the passages aloud and ask the patient to tell you "what this is all about." You can also design a few questions, four or five, to give you data on the main points.

For example, if the instruction says, "Avoid heavy lifting," ask the patient to give you an example of something he shouldn't lift. Similarly, if the instruction says, "Drink six glasses of fluid a day," ask the patient for an example of a "fluid" and inquire about what kinds of fluids he would drink.

It is a good idea to break out units of time from the instruction and ask separate questions. For example, "a day" may be confusing. Some people work a split shift or night shift and wonder if a day pertains only to daylight hours, or they may wonder if they have to set an alarm clock in order to take medicine on a 24-hour basis.

If you are pretesting material that consists of a description of a disease process or of a body function, ask the patient to tell you **in his own words** what the passage is all about. Remember what we said earlier about the test for comprehension as the ability to transform or change information from one format to another? Until the patient can tell you the key points in his own words, chances are that he only partially understands it.

Visuals

If you are pretesting material that has several pictures of a procedure or of a sequence, have the patient tell you what is going on in each picture and what the main point is. You might say something like, "Tell me what this picture shows." You might follow up with something like, "Is this a good picture of what you would really do?" Any clues of how the patient would change it are important to record for possible revision of your material.

Visuals With Text

Test to be sure that the patient associates the text or the caption with the visual. Sometimes the caption points out only one part of the visual, such as storing household cleaning fluids on shelves out of the reach of children. The reader may see other details in the visual and miss the point. The caption should make it clear to the reader what the main point is in the visual.

Lists, such as diet exchange lists, may be very difficult for people with low literacy skills. Concepts of choice and substitution are critical messages from your point of view. But consider the patient's viewpoint. If he is confronted with a bewildering array of something like 22 fruits of different amounts and sizes as well as 29 vegetables that also vary in amount if they are used cooked, raw, fresh, frozen, or canned, he may just collapse in a pile of details. In a case like this, pretest only the essential foods. For example, after you have found out what the patient likes to eat and have checked his diet prescription, take a felt-tip pen or a pencil and circle the foods on the list that are O.K. for him to eat.

Personalize the list. For foods that are clearly "off limits," use a separate sheet of paper marked, *"Do not eat these foods."* Using lower case printing, write the names of the foods that are the biggest offenders. As you do this, have the patient talk with you and say each of the foods out loud. Many patients with low literacy skills do not read cursive or longhand. Avoid ALL CAPITALS, *light italics*, and script. These patients need the different sizes and shapes of letters to distinguish one letter from another.

Units of measurement may be unfamiliar to your patient. Such units of measurement as teaspoon, tablespoon, servings of meat, fish, and other foods, and fractions of ½ and ¼ all have to be tested.

Have cups, spoons, or rulers with you when you pretest units of measurement so that the patient can select and show you the amount he understands the portion to be.

If you are pretesting material on exercises for arthritic patients, have the patients demonstrate the exercise if at all possible. If, after they look at the drawing and read most of the text, they can perform the exercise, you can be reasonably certain that the message has come across.

Audio Tapes

If you are pretesting tapes, prepare several questions that relate to the main purpose of the tape. Play only 2 or 3 minutes of the tape at a time because the memory load is heavy. Did the patient follow the directions given in the tape? For example, when asked to turn the tape off and respond, did the patient do this? If it is a slide-tape, find out if the patient associated the visual with the audio in the manner you intended. Did the picture help or hinder? Did the mechanics of operating the tape recorder or other equipment cause trouble for the patient?

Time-Related Information

Pretest to make certain that the patient comprehends the specifics of time-related information. Sometimes we take the obvious for granted and that's when we get into trouble. As we've mentioned before, many people with low literacy skills may not know the months of the year, the days of the week, or how morning and afternoon are written (AM and PM). As we encounter more and more people for whom English is a second language, the problem becomes even more widespread.

If the patient is to take medication at mealtime, make sure he understands if it is to be taken before, with, or after meals. The term "at meal time" is too vague to be useful.

WHEN DO YOU PRETEST?

There are several stages when you can pretest your material. You may elect to run a check (Bertrand, 1978).

At the concept stage. Try out your idea via a storyboard as we described in Chapter 6 so that you can get an evaluation of the concept before it is fully developed.

At the partially completed stage. Present a rough draft to find out what changes might be made before you go any further.

To test alternative versions. Produce several different versions to determine which one is potentially most effective. When you're not sure of a sketch or illustration, pretest it along with another version to find out which one works best.

To test the final product. Once you have produced it, you may need a final test before your material becomes official. You need not have the finished version with final art, printing, and binding to ensure the usefulness of your material. There is evidence to show that materials in preliminary

form yield similar results to tests of the same
material in final form. Simulate size, color, type
print, and lay out in your final trial version. This
advice is especially important if you are planning
a large national distribution.

WHERE DO YOU PRETEST?

Natural settings under realistic conditions are the best
testing grounds. You may get results faster and have greater
control if you arrange a setting or room, but the disadvantage is
that respondents are aware that they are being observed and
may give extraordinary attention to the material, thereby
giving you misleading data. You are also less likely to get the
personal response of the patient.

HOW LARGE SHOULD THE
SAMPLE FOR PRETESTING BE?

Two general rules should be kept in mind: (1) the larger
the sample size, the more confidence you can have in the
results; (2) it is better to have some feedback, even from a very
small sample, than to have no feedback at all.

In general, if the intended audience is fairly homogeneous,
a total of 25 to 50 respondents should be selected. If the
intended audience is very heterogenous, then 15 to 20 respondents from each major subgroup, such as age, sex, or ethnic
composition, or from at least the two largest subgroups should
be tested. There are no universal guidelines. Pretesting with 10
to 15 patients, carefully selected to be representative of your
patient population, is far better than no pretesting at all.

For many pretesting situations, random sampling may not
be possible and sample sizes may be small so that statistical
formulas may not be practical. Commercial advertising firms
usually use samples of 50 to 200 people for a given communication, though this number is often much higher, especially for
pretesting on a national scale.

HOW MUCH TIME DOES PRETESTING TAKE?

You should be able to conduct a pretest and interpret the results within a short period of time. It may take a few minutes for a simple instruction or up to a half hour for a complete piece.

WHO SHOULD BE INCLUDED IN THE PRETESTING SAMPLE?

Choose typical patients from your agency or institution who are going to use the material you produce. Try to include the key family members who influence the patient. For example, if you are pretesting prenatal instructions and you know that the husband or grandmother wields considerable influence with the patient, include these influential husbands or grandmothers in the sample. Key people in the patient's support system need to comprehend and accept the message just as much as the patient does. **A word of caution:** do not use staff members, even entry-level aides, as a sounding board instead of patients. They are likely to be more familiar with what you are trying to say than is the patient and they may respond to please or to tease you. Staff members are very useful in the concept stage and in sharing ideas on content, but they do not function well as test subjects.

WHO DOES THE PRETESTING?

You do. The person who gives the instruction needs to be the one who is finding out about its usefulness.

Here are a few more "don'ts" and words of caution: don't delegate this task to a secretary or clerk or send it in the mail to another office to handle. We used a network of sites for pretesting a handbook on medical care for seafarers. Despite detailed instructions on how to conduct the pretest, each site carried out the instructions in its own way. In several locations, only those who could read or write were included in the sample.

The most critical part of the population was thereby missed—those who could only take a listening test.

It may seem that we are belaboring the point, but don't attempt to use any kind of self-administered pretest with adults having low literacy skills. There are several reasons for this (Bertrand, 1978):

☐ The results have little validity if the target audience has difficulty reading and writing.

☐ Respondents will tend to skip over difficult items, leaving you with incomplete information.

☐ Respondents may go back and change their answers to earlier questions after reading other items, or they may read the whole pretest before answering any items. Then the pretest serves as a training device.

WHAT KINDS OF MEDIA CAN BE PRETESTED?

All kinds. Films and film strips can be pretested in the storyboard format before production. Radio and television spots can be pretested in script form or taped so that the patient can listen. You can follow with an interview in person after the patient listens to the tape. Full-length programs can be pretested in script form.

Posters, pamphlets, instruction sheets, and throw-aways as well as slide tapes can all be pretested. If you are using two types of media, for example, slide/tapes, check on the synchronization as well as on the messages coming through with each medium.

WHAT KINDS OF CHANGES RESULT FROM PRETESTING?

Notice how pretesting changed the wording on the instructions for men who had prostate surgery (see Home Care Instructions for Men Who Had a Prostate Operation).

Home Care Instructions for Men Who Had a Prostate Operation

Before Pretest	*After Pretest*
1. Be sure you get an appointment for follow-up care.	1. **No change**
2. Avoid walking up and down stairs for at least two weeks after discharge.	2. Do not walk up and down stairs for at least two weeks after discharge.
3. Avoid excessive strain, especially sex, for 6 to 8 weeks after surgery.	3. **No change but add:** Changing a flat tire, running, reaching, or getting up too fast are examples of excessive strain.
4. Avoid heavy lifting.	4. Do not lift anything you cannot pick up easily.
5. Drink about 6 glasses of fluid per day. Do most of the drinking during the day.	5. Drink about 6 glasses of fluid during a 24-hour period. Do most of the drinking during waking hours. Water, tea, coffee, milk, juice, soda, and clear soups count as fluids.
6. For constipation, take a laxative, for instance, milk of magnesia, but do *not* use a suppository.	6. **No change**
7. Do not drink alcoholic beverages for 3 weeks after discharge.	7. **No change but add:** Alcoholic beverages include wine, beer, whiskey, gin, rum, vodka, and cordials.

(continued)

Home Care Instructions for Men Who Had a Prostate Operation (*continued*)

Before Pretest	*After Pretest*
8. If chills, fever, testicular pain, or excessive bleeding from the penis occur, call the Urology Secretary, 447-3010, ext. 396.	8. If chills, fever, testicular pain, or any bleeding from the penis occurs, call the hospital operator, 447-3010. There is always a urologist on call.
9. Ask the doctor or nurse if you have any questions about how to take care of yourself while at home.	9. **No change**

Discussion of Changes*

Generalized terms, such as "excessive" or "heavy," need to have examples. "Heavy" may mean 20 to 25 pounds to one man, but the weight may differ for another. The examples used in the text came from the patients and were reviewed by the clinic staff.

One key point that the staff would not have picked up without the pretest was whom to call for help. The patients couldn't understand why they should talk to a secretary if they had bleeding from the penis. What the instruction meant was that the secretary would get in touch with the urologist, but the information was much clearer when it stated specifically whom to call and that there is always a urologist on call.

Chills, fever, and pain were clear enough, but what is "excessive bleeding"? One man said it was dripping as opposed to oozing; another said it depended on the color, that is, bright

*Skiff A: A Pretest of Written Material. Process and Outcome. USPHS Hospital, State Island, N.Y. Clinic Directors Conference, Houston, Texas, September 27, 1978

red blood as contrasted to brown tinges; another said he'd go by trial and error. If he saw a little blood once, that would be O.K., but if he saw it again, he would be worried. With this range of opinion, the professional staff eliminated the term "excessive bleeding" and inserted the phrase "any bleeding."

Most of the patients had a limited notion of the wide range of fluids or liquids available to them. Tea and coffee were seldom mentioned in fluid count. One man asked how you could drink during the day if you worked on the night shift. About half of the patients tested did not consider wines or beer as alcoholic beverages.

While it is important to pretest the message itself, it is also important to pretest the way the message is transmitted. In the Florida pap smear program for certain groups of welfare recipients the message was carefully pretested, but it was **mailed in an envelope** that said "Cancer Control Demonstration Project." All of the women in a large housing project boycotted the program because they perceived the "Demonstration Project" as a form of sterilization.

CAN MATERIALS BE TRANSFERRED FROM ONE PART OF THE COUNTRY TO ANOTHER?

It's highly questionable that results of testing apply to all geographical areas. Although comprehension may be satisfactory, acceptance may not. For example, the Cancer Control Program of the Public Health Service attempted to use a slide-tape series with physicians and found that tapes produced in Boston were not acceptable in Vermont. Tapes produced in Alabama were useful primarily within that state, and occasionally in Georgia and Tennessee. They were marginally acceptable in North Carolina.

Does this factor operate with patients of low literacy skills? Probably, because it appears to be true of all groups in society. Visual aids on malaria produced by the World Health Organization and used successfully in Nigeria were slated to be used in the Congo. However, before distribution a pretest was conducted with the material in the Congo (Courtejoie and Herman, 1965). Two important differences emerged: first, the Congo group did not perceive the sequence of the procedures with the same logic as the Nigerians did. Although they understood the same facts, they didn't assimilate the information in the same way. Second, they did not identify with the people pictured in the material. "We don't live like that in our villages," they said, and therefore they rejected the message. The paradox is that they did live in the same type house, but the women in the Congo wanted to be pictured using the more modern galvanized buckets rather than the old fashioned calabashes.

Another problem occurred with posters for malaria control showing a greatly magnified mosquito. The people laughed, "Who ever saw a mosquito that big?" Rely on the judgment of your own patient population because the logic and experiences of another group can produce different perceptions and comprehension.

CAN PRETESTING LEAD TO OTHER ACTIVITIES?

Yes indeed. The Los Angeles Cancer Education Project pretested national and local publications with a group of potential users from the Hispanic community. The group found the material not suitable for their community and decided to revise and rewrite it for themselves (Curry, 1976). Before long, they were so stimulated by their activity that they were willing to share responsibilities, not only for editing and discussing material, but also for leading community discussion sessions on cancer. By the end of the first year, *Hablaremos Sobre Cancer Dentro de la Familia* (Let's Talk About Cancer Among the Family) was published, an ingenious extended family distribution system was developed, and effective evaluation was completed.

SUMMARY

Feedback from pretesting your material tells you whether your patients understand the message that you intend. Pretesting will improve efficiency, is not time-consuming, and will give you additional clues to improve the comprehension process. Such clues may range from simple word changes to conceptual changes requiring additional illustrations and text.

Patients can become partners in the communication process, and message-testing is a legitimate useful activity to strengthen this relationship.

REFERENCES

Bertrand JT: Designing a Pretest, pp 13–20. Communications Pretesting, Media Monograph 6. Chicago, IL, Communications Laboratory, Community and Family Study Center, University of Chicago, 1978

Courtejoie J, Herman F: Producing visual aids in Central Africa. International Journal of Health Education 8, no. 4:174–178, 1965

Curry VM: Mexican American Cancer Education Project. Los Angeles County Branch, Division of the American Cancer Society. Written for the Upjohn Health Education Project, 1976, Making Health Education Work. Washington, DC, American Public Health Association, 1976

BIBLIOGRAPHY

Audiovisual Communication Handbook. A World Neighbors Publication, 5116 No. Portland Avenue, Oklahoma City, OK 73112. Compiled and edited by Dennis W. Pett. Originally developed under Peace Corps Contract 25-1707, Audio Visual Center, Indiana University, Bloomington, Ind. 47401

Pretesting in Health Communications: Methods, Examples, and Resources for Improving Health Messages and Materials. NIH Pub. No. 81-1493 (Rev. Nov. 1980) U.S. Department of Health and Human Services, PHS, NIH, NCI, Bethesda, MD 20205

Sticht T: Reading for Working: A Functional Literacy Anthology. Alexandria, VA, Human Resources Research Organization, 1975

CHAPTER TEN
Learning Disabilities

Up to this point, we've discussed health instruction methods for patients who have limited literacy **skills.** Another category of patients who need special instructional methods are those with learning disabilities.

Learning disabilities may prevent some patients from understanding even the most carefully designed health instruction. This chapter highlights some of these learning disabilities and discusses how to recognize them and what can be done by health professionals to cope with them.

LEARNING DISABILITY—A PROBLEM WITH MANY FACETS

A person who has a learning disability may suffer from more than just an inability to read. There may be many other related problems that interfere with learning. Some learning-disabled persons will miss appointments because their sense of time is inaccurate. Because of spacial disorientation, some will have difficulty following directions and will get lost going from one section of the hospital to another. Some will become very confused if given more than one direction at a time, and many will have considerable difficulty in reading written information or in remembering what is said.

The smallest things, inconsequential to most people, can interfere with learning. A clock with a swinging pendulum or a curtain moving in the breeze in a room where they are being advised can so distract some people that they lose any message they have been given. If there is an auditory defect, the sound of traffic or a lawn mower or corridor noise may distract the patient so that your message is lost.

Some learning-disabled persons fidget incessantly. If they

know this and try not to fidget, their effort to control their movements may drain all their energy and they may have none left to devote to learning. Even such simple tasks as unscrewing the cap on a bottle may be a trial-and-error affair for some. They can't remember which way the cap should be turned and thus may tighten the cap that they want to remove. Add this confusion to the problems many of us have with child-proof bottles and the result may be high frustration.

But the most important concern that you may face is the difficulty a learning-disabled person may experience in following directions. If the directions are in written form, the patient may not admit that he cannot read or that he cannot remember what he reads. If there is a critical sequence in a series of tasks to be performed, such as breathing exercises, the learning-disabled patient may reverse the sequence without realizing it. A nested set of measuring cups may result in a serving that was not intended in the diet prescription because the patient was confused about the cup size.

General and nonspecific instructions may be totally impossible for a learning disabled person who needs firm, unequivocal guidelines. Conditional phrases such as "when you are irregular," "as often as needed," "if you overeat," "whenever you can," or "don't worry if you miss taking your medicine occasionally" are so vague as to be meaningless to some learning-disabled patients. They may indeed worry; or they may go to the other extreme and take the vagueness as a license to ignore the need for regular compliance altogether.

For learning-disabled patients particularly, you must say what you mean and mean what you say. You must give a message more than one way and guarantee understanding, at least in the short-term, by having the patient repeat or demonstrate what is to be understood.

WHAT CAUSES LEARNING DISABILITIES?

Why is it that people who otherwise may appear bright and competent may lack the skills that medical advisors regard as simple? There is, as yet, no fully agreed upon way to diagnose, explain, or treat all learning disabilities. For some people, a genetic factor appears to be at work. For others, some central nervous system injury, a high fever in childhood, an accident, or some evidence of tissue trauma is a suspected cause.

Developmental lag is also suspect. The usual milestones of development have not occurred at a time when instruction is provided which presumes that development has taken place. For example, although phonic instruction in the schools is emphasized in first and second grade, some children seem to lack the auditory awareness of sound differences until a later stage in their development. By the time they are ready, the instructional program has already left them behind.

There are some who even deny that there is such a thing as a learning disability. For these people, inadequate learning is the result of inadequate teaching. But anyone who has ever watched a bright and motivated person struggle valiantly to do what most first-graders can do with ease and yet **fail** knows that learning disability is real and extremely painful to those who live with it.

RESEARCH ON DYSLEXIA

Research on dyslexia has been ongoing for over 50 years. *Dyslexia* is the popular term for a variety of learning-disabling symptoms. Steven Mattis of New York's Montefiore Hospital and Medical Center has identified four main types of language problems:

1. A problem in naming objects, for example, a clamp becomes a "holding thing"
2. Problems in the motor area so that smooth utterance is difficult. Speech is jumbled and syntax is often awkward.
3. Visual perceptual disorder that causes problems in recognizing similar letters, like n, h, and, of course, b and d, and words that reverse, like **saw** and **was**
4. Problems in speaking that cause a person to reproduce the sounds of words in the wrong order even though they hear them correctly. Such a person says "predisent" for "president" and "pisgetti" for "spaghetti."

Each of these difficulties seems to point to a neurologic basis for the anomaly. However, it has only been recently that **physical** evidence has been discovered that would seem to confirm the notion of a neurologic link. Conventional electroencephalographs (EEGs) have not been consistent as a diagnostic tool in the exploration of dyslexia.

Dr. Frank H. Duffy of Boston Children's Hospital combined the EEG with computer technology and produced what is called **brain electrical activity mapping** (BEAM), which delivers a colored picture of the brain in action. Dr. Duffy found that the BEAM patterns of dyslexics are significantly different from those of the normal population and that the differences are widely distributed throughout the brain system. He believes that the pattern of brain disruption that results in such varied behavior abnormalities is not caused by a discrete brain lesion, but is attributable to some more pervasive element.

Many dyslexics have been men of genius. Einstein, Edison, Nelson Rockefeller, Leonardo da Vinci, and Michelangelo all had various degrees of dyslexia. Many of the general population may have some symptoms but they are not sufficiently disrupting to cause trouble. Awareness of the limitations dyslexic individuals must struggle with has spawned a host of techniques and programs to correct the problem but as yet no certain "cures" are available.

DYSLEXIA IS A CONDITION, NOT A DISEASE

What seems important is to realize that dyslexia is not a disease; rather, it is a condition that results in a dysfunction of one or more of the language processes—listening, speaking, reading, or writing. It may relate to a central nervous system injury, to a developmental lag with resultant educational failure, or to constitutional differences that may have a genetic base. There are those who implicate diet, especially food additives, and even fluorescent lighting, but there is no supportive research for these theories.

Neurological research is likely to lead the way to a better understanding of the dyslexic individual, but it is unlikely that some form of medication will provide a complete remedy. At the present time, an adjustment in the form and process of our educational arrangements is the only helpful intervention.

How do we arrange such intervention? Although this book is full of suggestions, some additional comments, particularly geared to dyslexics, seem warranted.

WHAT WE KNOW—SUMMARIZED

1. Dyslexia is a condition describing those people who have a variety of language difficulties not associated with mental retardation, inadequate schooling, emotional disturbance, cultural deprivation, or inadequate visual or auditory acuity.
2. There are multiple symptoms that may be related to a variety of dysfunctions involving visual, auditory, or motor integration.
3. Not all dyslexics have the same symptoms nor do they display the same disabilities.
4. Although the problems are assumed to have a neurologic foundation, the mechanism that is faulty has not been identified, nor is there agreed-upon information as to why such anomalies occur.
5. At the present time, remediation is educational and involves developing compensatory competencies.
6. Dyslexia is a condition that continues to affect the individual throughout life, although those with high intelligence, social support, and strong personal motivation can demonstrate remarkable achievement. Many dyslexics are college graduates and many have distinguished themselves to a remarkable degree in fields less dependent on language.

TEACHING THOSE WITH A LEARNING DISABILITY

Among those who do not achieve language competence are many unremediated dyslexics as well as people whose academic failure is due to limited intelligence, inadequate schooling, cultural limitations, or unfortunate psychological histories. It is unlikely that you will be able to tell to which group a given patient may belong even if you could divide the readers from the nonreaders with some assurance. Fortunately, your objective is not to teach reading or spelling, but rather to teach the information, skills, and attitudes essential to the physical well-being of the patient. The dyslexic individual learns in the same way that anyone else learns—by first understanding the significant details and then using this information again and again until the action or the related facts become automatic.

The difference between dyslexic learning and the learning of the nondyslexic individual is that dyslexics, even more than slow-learning patients, may require more encounters. The messages need to be given through more than one sensory pathway (visual, auditory, kinesthetic, or tactile) before learning takes place. It may require some experimenting to discover what channel seems to work best. Sometimes a patient can tell you that. If you ask, "Can you remember best if you read something or if someone tells you something?" you may discover whether your patient is a visual or auditory learner, or you may be giving your patient an easy way to indicate his poor reading skills without embarrassment. In any case, good instruction will require variety.

This instructional variety and repetition can also be facilitating to nondyslexics who learn slowly. The following are some principles to remember:

1. As with any instruction, divide the information into essential and nonessential elements. Teach only what is essential.

2. Do not rely on written brochures or on oral instructions given only once. Show and tell, then listen and watch.

3. Do this in more than one way if you can. For example, when instructing on diet for weight control, teach one principle, then use food models or pictures to demonstrate. You may also use restaurant menus to provide more practice and market basket items to say it again in another way.

4. Keep patient choices and alternatives at a minimum until a routine has been established.

Introduce diversity slowly and one thing at a time.

5. Clutter of any kind—visual or auditory—is especially disturbing to the learning disabled. Sometimes it helps to box a statement or a picture you want them to learn. This serves to separate the key concept from other detail.

6. Perseveration is a problem with some learning-disabled persons. Like the phonograph needle stuck in a groove, they can't seem to move on. They may make an error and continue to repeat it, unable to change their behavior even though they know it is faulty. When that happens, it is best to change the activity and come back to the problem area another time.

7. People with learning disability may also be prone to be impulsive. They often respond before thinking. If a hasty reply shows evidence of little thought, be patient. Provide a suggestion or two to guide the patient in such a way that a more satisfactory response is forthcoming.

8. Remember, difficulty in organizing is the central problem for the learning disabled. Recognize this by supplying as much structure as you can, thus easing the load and facilitating learning.

9. Provide a setting for instruction that is as free from distractions as possible. Seat your patient so that he faces a blank wall, not an open window or a busy corridor. Speak slowly and allow time for the patient to take in what is said or shown.

10. Have your patient respond by retelling the given information. If he cannot, coach him. He may need to hear himself say it in order to learn. If there is a behavior the patient is to carry out, have him demonstrate it. If he cannot, coach him until he is successful and then let him demonstrate the entire sequence without your assistance. If possible, check

again for forgetting after a period of time has elapsed.

11. Provide assurance that your patient can call you if there is any question that needs an answer.

The many other suggestions in this book also apply to the learning disabled. Many will learn from tapes. Some will need to walk through a sequence more than once. Some will need to say the instructions as they do the sequence. All will be grateful if you will understand that their condition is one they would gladly change if they could.

With patience and understanding, you can both succeed.

BIBLIOGRAPHY

Bond GL, Tinker M: Reading Difficulties: Their Diagnosis and Correction. New York, Appleton-Century-Crofts, 1980

Houck C: Learning Disabilities: Understanding Concepts, Characteristics, and Issues. Englewood Cliffs, NJ, Prentice-Hall, 1974

Kaluger G, Kolson C: Reading and Learning Disabilities. Columbus, Ohio, Chas E Merrill, 1978

Lee G, Berger A: Learning Disabilities with Emphasis on Reading. Newark, DE, International Reading Association, 1978

Lerner JW: Children with Learning Disabilities, Boston, Houghton-Mifflin, 1980

Pediatric Annals 8, no. 11, 1979

Salvia J, Ysseldyke J: Assessment in Special and Remedial Education. Boston, Houghton-Mifflin, 1978

Stauffer RG, Abrams JC, Pikulski J: Diagnosis, Correction, and Prevention of Reading Disabilities. New York, Harper & Row, 1978

INDEX